Real-Life English

A COMPETENCY-BASED ESL PROGRAM FOR ADULTS

Program Consultants

Jayme Adelson-Goldstein
North Hollywood Learning Center
North Hollywood, California

Patricia De Hesus-Lopez
Texas A & M University
Kingsville, Texas

Julia Collins
Los Angeles Unified School District
El Monte-Rosemead Adult School
El Monte, California

Federico Salas-Isnardi
Houston Community College
Adult Literacy Programs
Houston, Texas

Else V. Hamayan
Illinois Resource Center
Des Plaines, Illinois

Connie Villaruel
El Monte-Rosemead Adult School
El Monte, California

Kent Heitman
Carver Community Middle School
Delray Beach, Florida

Wei-hua (Wendy) Wen
Adult & Continuing Education
New York City Board of Education
New York, New York

STECK-VAUGHN
COMPANY
A Subsidiary of National Education Corporation

◆ ACKNOWLEDGMENTS

Staff Credits:

Executive Editor	◆	Ellen Lehrburger
Senior Editor	◆	Tim Collins
Design Manager	◆	Richard Balsam
Cover Design	◆	Richard Balsam

Photo Credits:
Cover: © Randal Alhadeff, Cooke Photographics (title).

Illustration Credits:
The Ivy League of Artists, Inc.

Additional Illustration by:
Scott Bieser–p.62a-c, 62e-j, 63b, 63c, 63e, 63f, 63h, 63i, 63k, 63l, 63n, 63o, 64c-e, 65b-g, 67b, 69a, 69b, 69f-h, 69j, 70c, 70f, 70g, 70i, 70l, 71b, 71c, 71g-i, 72b, 72d, 72h, 74b, 75b, 75e, 77b, 83d; D. Childress–p.98d, 107e, 107f; Rhonda Childress–p.8c, 8d, 30a, 38b-d, 40c, 64a, 64b; Adolph Gonzalez–p.66c, 67a, 67c, 90c, 91c, 91f, 95b, 95f, 106, 144g, 149h, 150; David Griffin–p.76f-j, 76l, 76m, 81b, 81d, 81f, 81h, 83f, 83g, 122a-h, 122j-l, 123, 128a, 130, 131a-d, 146; Lyda Guz–p.48d; John Harrison–p.74c-e, 75a, 75c, 75d, 76b-e, 76k-m, 81f, 83b, 83c, 83e-g, 90b, 90d-g, 91a, 91b, 91d, 91e, 91g, 91h, 91j-m, 95a, 95c-e, 96a, 96b, 96e, 96g, 96h, 98a, 99a-c, 107a-c, 122c, 122i, 144c, 144d, 144f, 145, 149a-g, 149i ; Michael Krone–p.12, 14, 16, 18, 50a, 52, 54, 56; Yvette Scott–p.112; Keith Wilson–p.8a, 8b, 23, 32d, 32e, 38a, 40a, 40b, 40d, 42, 44a, 44b, 45a-e, 47a, 47b, 48c, 66a, 72a, 74a, 75f, 78, 80, 83a, 88, 90a, 96c, 96d, 99d, 100-104, 107d, 108, 110, 111, 114, 120, 127a.

About The Writer:
Sarah Cogliano holds a B.A. degree from Wellesley College, Wellesley, Massachusetts. She has taught ESL/EFL to adults in Guadalajara, Mexico, Boston, Massachusetts, and Austin, Texas. Ms. Cogliano currently specializes in materials development for ESL and Adult Basic Education.

Electronic Production:
International Electronic Publishing Center, Inc.

CONTENTS

Real-Life English is a complete competency-based, four-skill program for teaching ESL to adults and young adults. *Real-Life English* follows a competency-based syllabus that is compatible with the CASAS and MELT competencies, as well as state curriculums for adult ESL from Texas and California. The program is designed for students enrolled in public or private schools, learning centers, or institutes, and for individuals working with tutors.

The program consists of four levels plus this Literacy Level. The Literacy Level is intended for use with students who have no prior knowledge of English and few or no literacy skills in their own language(s). It is also designed for use with students who are literate in a language with a non-Roman alphabet. Because unit topics carry over from other levels of *Real-Life English,* the Literacy Level can be used prior to or with Level 1.

Real-Life English has these components:

♦ Five Student Books (Literacy and Levels 1–4).

♦ Five Teacher's Editions (Literacy and Levels 1–4), which provide detailed suggestions on how to present each section of the Student Book in class.

♦ Four Workbooks (Levels 1–4), which provide reinforcement for each section of Student Books 1–4.

♦ Two Audiocassettes at each level (Literacy and Levels 1–4), which contain all dialogs and listening activities in the Student Books. ⊡ This symbol indicates all of the activities for which material is recorded on the Audiocassettes. A transcript of all material recorded on the tapes but not appearing directly on the Student Book pages is at the back of each Student Book and Teacher's Edition.

Organization of the Literacy Level Student Book

Real-Life English Literacy Level consists of a ten-page Introductory Unit and ten units of instruction. The competencies for each unit are listed by unit in the Table of Contents. Teachers can use this list for lesson planning and for learner verification.

Introductory Unit

The Introductory Unit presents left-to-right progression, top-to-bottom progression, number formation, letter formation, letter discrimination and capital/lower case letter correspondence. In addition, the Introductory Unit uses captioned pictures to present the direction lines in the rest of the book. A page lined with wide (primary) rules is also provided for teachers and/or students to duplicate and use for additional writing practice. (Teachers can also use copies of this page to create their own worksheets. Write the words, letters, or sentences students need to practice on a copy of the page. Then duplicate it for students.)

The Introductory Unit can be used in several ways. Teachers can present any or all of the pages before students begin Unit 1. Or teachers might have students turn back to these pages for extra reinforcement as the class works through each unit. Because the Introductory Unit can be used at any point in the book, *Real-Life English* Literacy Level is ideal for open-entry/open-exit programs.

Units 1–10

Units 1–10 follow a competency-based syllabus that presents foundation literacy skills in tandem with listening and speaking skills. Thus, students simultaneously develop the language and life skills they need to live in the U.S.

The *About You* symbol, a unique feature, appears on the Student Book page each time students use a competency independently.

Blackline Masters and Listening Transcript

At the end of the book, Blackline Masters for each unit allow for valuable reinforcement and enrichment of instruction. The Listening Transcript presents all of the listening activities not appearing directly on the Student Book pages.

Organization of a Unit

Each of the ten units follows a consistent whole-part-whole organization:

♦ The Unit Opener presents an overview of the unit topic and competencies.

♦ Four to five teaching spreads systematically present the new material in the unit.

♦ The Put It Together, Check Your Competency, and Extension pages allow for integration, evaluation, and expansion of the new language and competencies.

Unit Opener

Each Unit Opener of *Real-Life English* Literacy Level includes a large, engaging illustration and accompanying questions. Each illustration depicts people using the unit's target language, literacy skills, and competencies. Situations include people applying for jobs, completing forms, shopping for food or clothing, finding homes, or seeing doctors. The illustration and questions activate students' prior knowledge by getting them to think and talk about the unit topic. To stimulate discussion, follow these suggestions:

♦ Encourage students to say whatever they can about the illustration. Prompt them by indicating objects for them to name. You

might also identify and say the names of objects, places, and people for them to repeat. Write key words on the board.

♦ Help students read any signs or words that are visible.

♦ Have students answer the questions. Repeat their answers or restate them in acceptable English.

Teaching Spreads

Each of the four to five teaching spreads presents one or more literacy and life skills. *Real-Life English* Literacy Level takes a recognition-word approach to teach letters, words, and competencies in meaningful, communicative contexts. Students learn to read and write only the words that they need to know to accomplish the unit competencies.

♦ The recognition words for each spread are presented at the top of the first page of each spread. For information on presenting recognition words, see "Presenting Recognition Words" on page vii.

♦ The first activity on each spread is a short dialog that presents recognition words in context. As students listen to and say each dialog, they gain valuable experience using the new language. For detailed instructions, see "Presenting Dialogs" on page vii.

♦ Exercises give students experience in reading and writing the recognition words in isolation and in context.

♦ The complete alphabet is presented in the first five units in groups of one or two letters on each spread. The letters are always the initial letters of the spread's recognition words. Thus, learning the alphabet becomes a meaningful, relevant task. Exercises give students experience in writing the letters in isolation and in familiar contexts. For suggestions on teaching the letters, see "Presenting Letters" on page vii.

♦ Listening and speaking activities appear on all the spreads, allowing students to develop all four language skills. The paired speaking activities get students talking from the start. Listening tasks include listening for addresses, telephone numbers, prices, directions, and doctors' instructions.

All of the listening activities develop the skill of **focused listening.** Students learn to recognize the information they need and listen selectively for only that information. They do not have to understand every word; rather, they have to filter out everything except the information that they want to find out. This essential skill is used by native speakers of all languages when listening in their own language.

♦ Culminating activities on each spread allow students to use their new literacy skills to read or fill in a piece of realia, such as a job application, a supermarket ad, a check, a receipt, a help-wanted ad, or a bus sign.

Put It Together

The communicative, integrative activities on the Put It Together page allow students to use the new language and competencies for the unit in a holistic reading/writing activity, such as reading a sale ad, completing a job application, reading medicine package labels, and writing checks.

Check Your Competency

The Check Your Competency page is designed to allow teachers to track students' progress and to meet their school's or program's learner verification needs. Skills are tested in the same manner that they were presented in the units, so formats are familiar and non-threatening, and success is built in. For more information on this section, see "Evaluation" on page vii.

Extension

The Extension page enriches the previous instruction with language puzzles, games, and other activities. As students complete these enjoyable activities, they gain additional experience in using the unit's target language and competencies.

Placement

Any number of measures can be used to place students in the appropriate level of *Real-Life English.* This table indicates placement based on the CASAS and MELT-SPL standards.

Student Performance Levels	CASAS Achievement Score	*Real-Life English*
	164 or under	Literacy
I	165–185	Level 1
II	186–190	
III	191–196	Level 2
IV	197–205	
V	206–210	Level 3
VI	211–216	
VII	217–225	Level 4
VIII	226 (+)	

Using this Book in Multi-Level Classes

Real-Life English Literacy Level can be used in a variety of ways in multi-level classes. Here is a suggested procedure.

♦ Present to the class as a whole the oral and aural activities for the day in Level 1 of *Real-Life English.*

♦ Meet with the literacy students as a group for their reading and writing practice as the Level 1 students complete the exercises in their Student Books and Workbooks.

♦ When the literacy students are ready to begin the independent or paired activities in their books, check the Level 1 students' work or provide them with additional instruction.

Teaching Techniques

Presenting Dialogs

To present the dialogs, follow these suggested steps.

♦ Establish meaning by having students talk about the illustration. Clarify all the new vocabulary in the dialog using pictures and pantomime.

♦ Play the tape or say the dialog aloud two or more times.

♦ Say the dialog aloud line-by-line for students to repeat chorally and then individually.

♦ Have students say the dialog together in pairs.

♦ Have several pairs say the dialog aloud for the class.

Presenting Recognition Words

To present each recognition word, first clarify the meaning of the word. Display the object or a picture card, or use the picture on the Student Book page. Say the word and have students repeat. Then display a word card with the word on it. Say the word. As you say it, sweep your hand under the word. Have students repeat. Call attention to the initial letter. Display the word card and the picture card at random and have the class say or read the word chorally each time. Continue until the class can respond with ease. Then have individuals respond.

Reinforcing Vocabulary

To provide additional reinforcement of the recognition words, use any of these suggestions.

♦ **Personal picture dictionaries.** Students can start personal dictionaries in their notebooks. For each new word they can draw or glue in a picture of the object or action.

♦ **Flash cards.** Flash cards are easy for teachers or for students to make. Write a new word or phrase on the front of each card. Put a picture of the object or action on the back of the card. Students can use the cards to review vocabulary or to play a variety of games, such as Concentration.

♦ **The Remember-It Game.** Use this simple memory game to review vocabulary of any topic. For example, to reinforce food words, start the game by saying, *We're having a picnic, and we're bringing apples.* The next student has to repeat what you said and add an item. If someone cannot remember the whole list or cannot add a word, he or she has to drop out. The student who can remember the longest list wins.

Presenting Letters

Use letter cards with both capital and lower-case letters on them to present the letters. Hold up each card, say the name of the letter, and have students repeat. Point out the difference between capital and lower-case letters. Write the capital and lower-case letters on the board and trace them with your finger. Have students trace the strokes in the air. Next have students open their books and trace the letters with their fingers and then with their pencils. Then have them write the letters on the lines.

Presenting Listening Activities

Use any of these suggestions to present the listening activities.

♦ Help students read the directions and the example.

♦ Model the activity. Write the example item on the board and complete it as you play the tape or read the Listening Transcript of the first item aloud. In activities in which students listen and raise their hands, model raising your hand as students observe.

- ♦ Play the tape or read the Listening Transcript aloud as students complete the activity. Rewind the tape and play it again as necessary.

- ♦ Check students' work.

Evaluation

To use the Check Your Competency page successfully, follow these suggested procedures. Before and during each evaluation, create a relaxed, affirming atmosphere. Chat with the students for a few minutes and review the material with them. When you and the students are ready, help students read the directions and look over each exercise before they complete it. Make sure that everyone has a pen or a pencil. Then have students complete the activity. If at any time during the process you sense that students are becoming frustrated, feel free to stop the evaluation process to provide additional review. You might have students turn back to the page where the material was presented. Resume when students are ready. Check students' work. The Teacher's Edition contains reproducible charts for you to copy and use to keep track of individual and class progress.

Introductory Unit

Start
➤

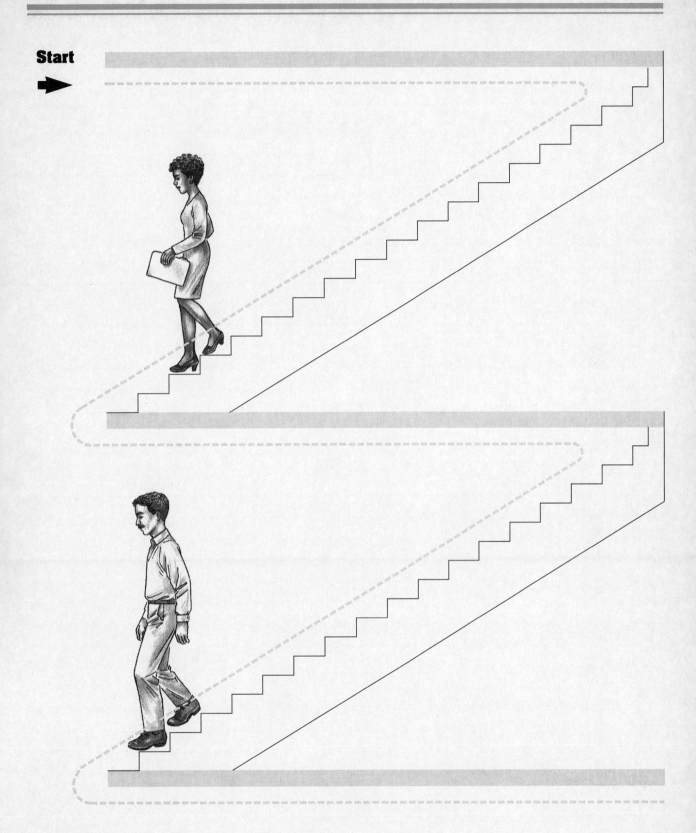

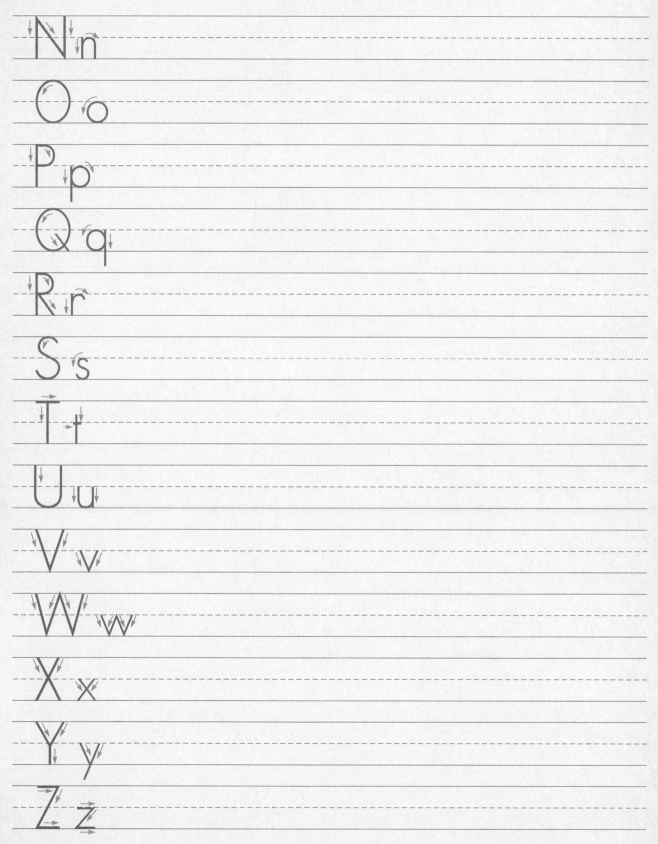

0

1

2

3

4

5

6

7

8

9

10

11

12

13

14

15

16

17

18

19

20

30

40

50

60

70

80

90

o	Ⓞ	a	e	c	Ⓞ
a	a	p	d	a	o
e	c	e	e	o	e
g	d	g	p	q	g
s	z	s	z	s	z
f	l	f	k	t	f
h	b	h	h	d	n
l	j	i	l	l	i
k	x	k	k	x	h
m	r	m	n	m	h

A	Ⓐ	I	H	H	Ⓐ
C	D	O	C	C	G
O	Q	O	O	C	D
U	U	W	V	U	V
M	M	A	M	N	M
P	R	D	P	P	R
S	Z	S	S	J	U
E	E	L	F	E	H
J	U	J	I	J	A
B	P	B	B	D	D

A	a c e	B	d b e
E	a c e	L	l i t
G	i g j	T	t i l
N	m r n	W	v w u

1. Listen.

2. Look.

3. Raise your hand.

4. Say.

8

5. Circle.

6. Underline.

7. Write.

8. Work with a partner.

Personal Communication

Look at the picture.

Where are the people?

What are they doing?

Name

1. Listen and practice the dialog.

 2. Your teacher writes your name.

Name: _____

You write your name.

Name: _____

Name: _____

Name: _____

Name: _____

Name: _____

Name: _____

3. Listen for name. **Raise your hand.**

4. Circle Name **and** NAME.

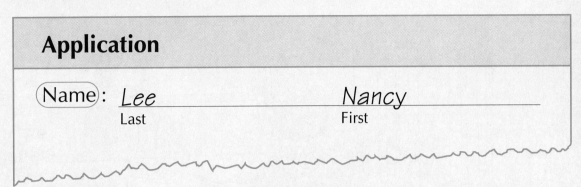

Application

(Name): *Lee*_____ *Nancy*_____
           Last   First

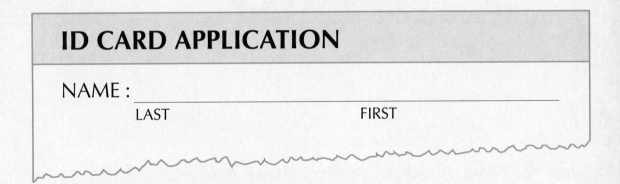

ID CARD APPLICATION

NAME : _____
           LAST   FIRST

5. Say the letters. Write the letters.

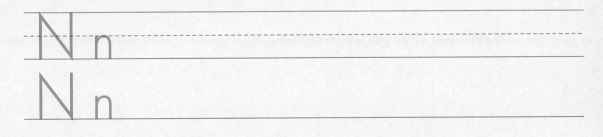

6. Write n. **Write your name. Say the sentence.**

About You

My _n_ame is _____ .

My ___ame is _____ .

My ___ame is _____ .

My ___ame is _____ .

1. Listen and practice the dialog.

➤ What's your first name?
● Nancy.
➤ What's your last name?
● Lee.

2. Your teacher writes your name.

Name: _____   _____
        First   Last

You write your name.

Name: _____   _____
        First   Last

Name: _____   _____
        First   Last

3. Listen. Circle the word you hear.

a. first   (last)

b. name   first

c. first   last

4. Circle Last, LAST, First, **and** FIRST.

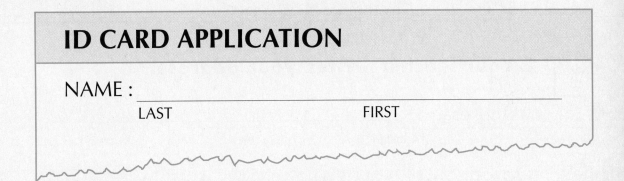

Application

Name : _____
       (Last)   ·   ·   First

ID CARD APPLICATION

NAME : _____
       LAST   FIRST

5. Write your name in 4.

6. Say the letters. Write the letters.

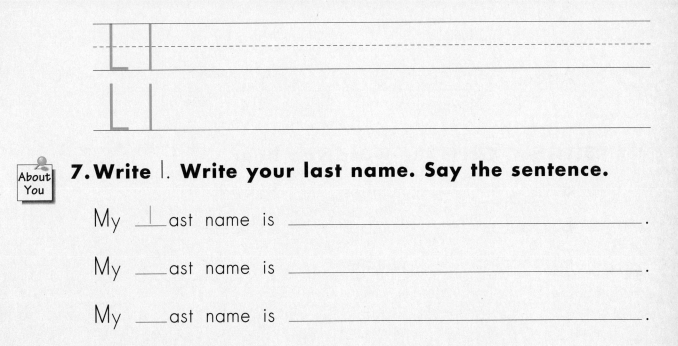

7. Write l. **Write your last name. Say the sentence.**

My ⌐ast name is _____ .

My ___ast name is _____ .

My ___ast name is _____ .

1. Listen and practice the dialog.

2. Your teacher writes your address.

Address: _____
           Number   Street

You write your address.

Address: _____
           Number   Street

Address: _____
           Number   Street

Address: _____
           Number   Street

3. Listen. Circle the word you hear.

a. (address)   number   street

b. address   number   street

c. address   number   street

4. Circle ADDRESS, Number, **and** Street.

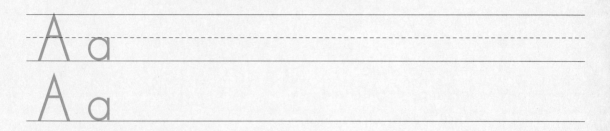

🎓 Monterey College Registration

NAME: *Hall*   *James*
  Last   First

(ADDRESS): *22*   *Pine Street*
  Number   Street

5. Say the letters. Write the letters.

Aa

Aa

6. Write A. **Write your address. Say your address.**

Address: _____
  Number   Street

___ddress: _____
  Number   Street

7. Write your name and address.

🍎 OAKLAND ADULT LEARNING CENTER

NAME: _____
  Last   First

ADDRESS: _____
  Number   Street

1. Listen and practice the dialog.

> ➤ What's your address?
> ● 22 Pine Street.
> ➤ City and state?
> ● Oakland, California.
> ➤ What's the zip code?
> ● 94610.

2. Your teacher writes your city, state, and zip code.

_____
CITY   STATE   ZIP CODE

You write your city, state, and zip code.

_____
CITY   STATE   ZIP CODE

_____
CITY   STATE   ZIP CODE

3. Listen for zip code. **Raise your hand.**

4. Circle City, State, **and** Zip Code.

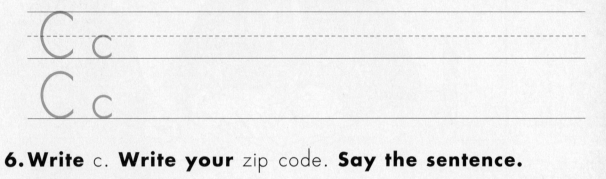

ADDRESS : ___22___ ___Pine Street___
             Number   **Street**

___Oakland___ ___California___ ___94610___
  (**City**)   **State**   **Zip Code**

5. Say the letters. Write the letters.

C c

C c

About You **6. Write** c. **Write your** zip code. **Say the sentence.**

My zip _c_ode is _____.

My zip ___ode is _____.

My zip ___ode is _____.

About You **7. Write your** city, state, **and** zip code.

ADDRESS : _____
            NUMBER   **STREET**

_____
       CITY   **STATE**   **ZIP CODE**

Telephone Number

1. Listen and practice the dialog.

 **2. Your teacher writes your telephone number.**

Telephone Number: _____

You write your telephone number.

Telephone Number: _____

Telephone Number: _____

Telephone Number: _____

📼 **3. Listen for telephone number. Raise your hand.**

4. Circle Telephone Number.

REGISTRATION CARD

Name:

Williams   Harold
<u>Last   First</u>

Telephone Number :

(510) 555-6311

Address:

35 Riverside Drive
<u>Number   Street</u>

Oakland California 94610
<u>City   State   Zip Code</u>

5. Say the letters. Write the letters.

T t

T t

6. Write t. **Write your telephone number. Say the sentence.**

My <u>t</u>elephone number is _____.

My ___elephone number is _____.

My ___elephone number is _____.

7. Complete the form.

REGISTRATION CARD

Name:

<u>Last   First</u>

Telephone Number:

Address:

<u>Number   Street</u>

<u>City   State   Zip Code</u>

◆ Put It Together

Make a class telephone list. Your classmates write their names and telephone numbers.

☎ CLASS TELEPHONE LIST ☎

Name:	Name:
Telephone Number:	Telephone Number:
Name:	Name:
Telephone Number:	Telephone Number:
Name:	Name:
Telephone Number:	Telephone Number:
Name:	Name:
Telephone Number:	Telephone Number:

Complete the form.

CITY LEARNING CENTER

NAME _____

               LAST   FIRST

TELEPHONE NUMBER (   ) _____

ADDRESS _____

               NUMBER   STREET

_____

               CITY   STATE   ZIP CODE

Extension

Circle the word.

1.	NAME	N A N A M E N E
2.	NAME	M A N E N A M E
3.	NAME	N E N A M E M E
4.	FIRST	F I R F I R S T
5.	FIRST	F F I R S T T F
6.	FIRST	S T F I R S T F
7.	LAST	L A L A S T L A
8.	LAST	L L A S T T L A
9.	LAST	L A S L A S T L

2 Our Community

Look at the picture.

Where are the people?

What are they doing?

1. Listen and practice the dialog.

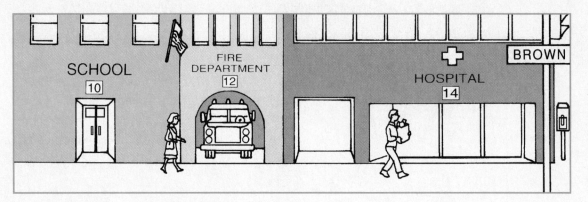

➤ Where's the hospital?
● 14 Brown Street.
➤ Where?
● 14 Brown Street.
➤ Thanks.

2. Work with a partner. Circle.

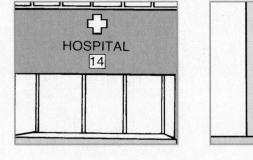 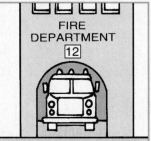 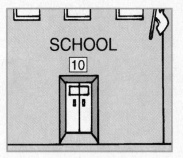

fire department   fire department   hospital
(hospital)   school   school

3. Say the letters. Write the letters.

Hh

Hh

4. Circle Fire Department **and** Hospital.
Underline the telephone numbers.

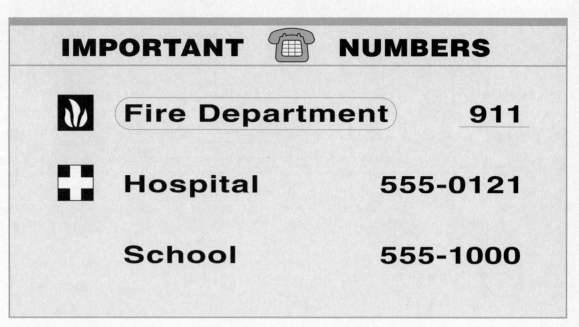

IMPORTANT 📞 **NUMBERS**

🔥 (Fire Department) <u>911</u>

✚ Hospital **555-0121**

School **555-1000**

5. Write h. **Say the words.**

<u>h</u>ospital   ___ospital   ___ospital

<u>h</u>ospital   ___ospital   ___ospital

sc<u>h</u>ool   sc___ool   sc___ool

sc<u>h</u>ool   sc___ool   sc___ool

About You

6. Work with a partner. Complete the chart.

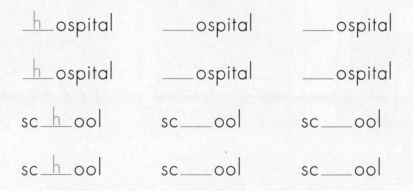

IMPORTANT 📞 NUMBERS	
Fire Department	
Hospital	
School	

Bank   Post Office   Police Station

1. Listen and practice the dialog.

➤ Where's the bank?
● It's on Green Street.
➤ Where?
● Green Street.
➤ Thanks.

2. Work with a partner. Circle.

police station   post office   post office

(bank)   bank   police station

3. Listen. Circle the place you hear.

a. bank   post office   (police station)

b. bank   post office   police station

c. bank   post office   police station

4. Say the letters. Write the letters.

P p

P p

O o

O o

5. Write p and o. Say the words.

p ost   o ffice   ___ost ___ffice   ___ost ___ffice

p ost   o ffice   ___ost ___ffice   ___ost ___ffice

p olice   ___olice   ___olice

p o lice   p ___lice   p ___lice

 6. Work with a partner. Complete the chart.

IMPORTANT  NUMBERS	
Fire Department	
Police	
Hospital	
School	

Stamp   Mailbox

1. Listen and practice the dialogs.

➤ Stamps, please.
● How many?
➤ Ten.
● OK.

➤ Where's the mailbox?
● Over there.

2. Work with a partner. Circle.

stamp

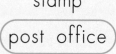
(post office)

stamp

mailbox

post office

stamp

3. Say the letters. Write the letters.

4. Write s, p, **and** o. **Say the words.**

_s_ tam _p_   ___ tam ___   ___ tam ___   ___ tam ___

mailb _o_ x   mailb ___ x   mailb ___ x   mailb ___ x

5. Listen. Circle the word you hear.

a. (post office)   stamp

b. stamps   mailbox

c. mailbox   stamp

About You

6. Write your name and address on the lines. Circle stamp.

Name _____	Place stamp here
Address _____	
NUMBER STREET	
_____	
CITY STATE ZIP CODE	

River City Bank

6 Green Street

River City, CA 98731

Fire   Accident   Ambulance

1. Listen and practice the dialogs.

➤ Hello. River City 911.
● Help! An accident!
  Send an ambulance.
➤ Where?
● Brown Street.

➤ Hello. River City 911.
● Help! A fire!
➤ Where?
● 6 Green Street.

2. Work with a partner. Circle.

fire
 accident

ambulance
accident

fire
ambulance

3. Say the letters. Write the letters.

F f

F f

4. Circle accident **and** fire.

5. Write f. **Say the word.**

f̲ire   ____ire   ____ire   ____ire

6. Work with a partner. Write the telephone numbers.

IMPORTANT	NUMBERS
Police	
Fire Department	
Ambulance	

Work with a partner.
Make a list of telephone numbers.

	NUMBER
Police	
Ambulance	
Fire Department	
School	
Post Office	
Bank	

I. Circle the word.

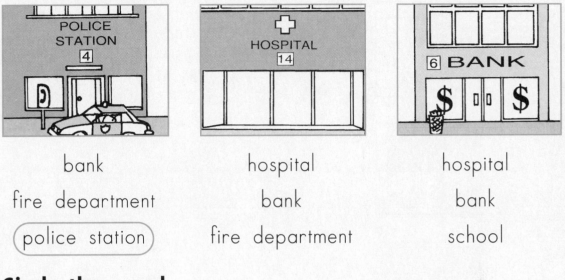

bank	hospital	hospital
fire department	bank	bank
(police station)	fire department	school

2. Circle the word.

(fire)	fire	school
accident	accident	fire department

3. Write the telephone numbers.

IMPORTANT ☎ NUMBERS	
Fire Department	
Police	
Ambulance	

◆◆◆ **Extension**

I. Write the word for each picture.

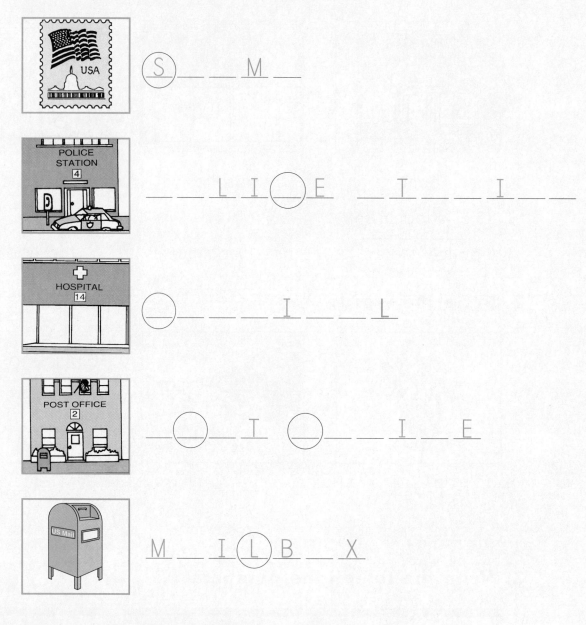

(S) _ _ M _

_ _ L I (_) E _ T _ _ I _ _

(_) _ _ I _ L

(_) _ T (_) _ I _ E

M _ I (L) B _ X

2. Write the circled letters on the lines.

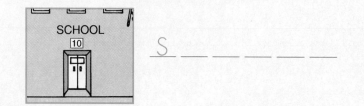

S _ _ _ _ _ _

School and Country

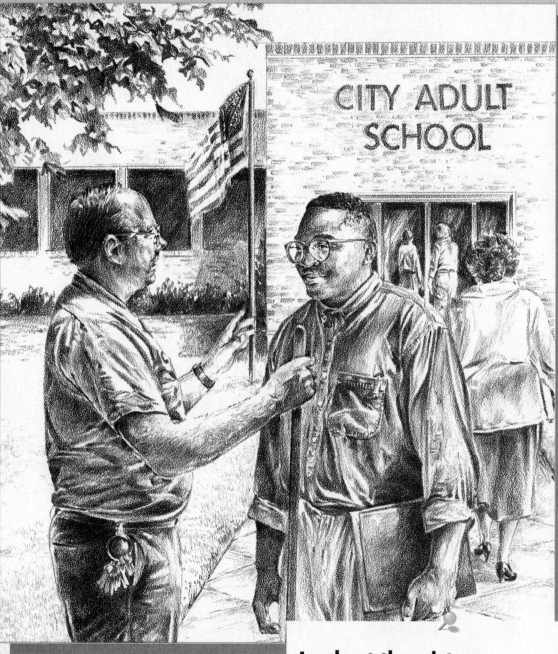

CITY ADULT
SCHOOL

Look at the picture.

Where are the people?

What are they doing?

Office   Library

1. Listen and practice the dialog.

➤ Where's the office?
● It's on the right, next to the library.
➤ On the right, next to the library?
● Yes.
➤ Thanks.

2. Look at the picture. Circle the word.

(school)   school   school
office   office   office
library   library   library

3. Say the letters. Write the letters.

4. Circle OFFICE **and** LIBRARY.
Underline the room numbers.

CITY ADULT SCHOOL

LIBRARY	12	TEACHERS' ROOM	22
(OFFICE)	<u>14</u>	MRS. HENDRICKS	24
MR. IGLESIAS	20	MR. KLEIN	30
MRS. YU	21	MS. PONTI	32

5. Write i. **Say the words.**

off_i_ce   off___ce   off___ce   off___ce

l_i_brary   l___brary   l___brary   l___brary

About You

6. Write i. **Answer the question about your school.**

➤ Where's the off___ce?

● It's next to _____.

About You

7. Work with a partner. Practice the dialog in 6.

1. Listen and practice the dialogs.

➤ I'm a new student.
  Who's my teacher?
● Mr. Klein.
➤ Thank you.

➤ Hello.
● What's your name?
➤ Pedro Montoya.
● What country are you from?
➤ Mexico.

**2. Work with a partner. Circle the student.
Underline the teacher.**

3. Say the letters. Write the letters.

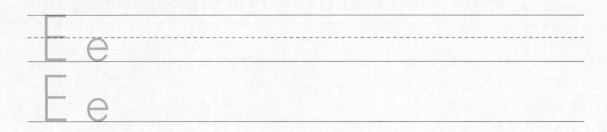

E e

E e

4. Circle TEACHER, STUDENT, **and** COUNTRY.

STUDENT : _Pedro Montoya_

COUNTRY : _Mexico_

(TEACHER) : _Mr. Klein_   LEVEL: _1_

CITY ADULT SCHOOL

Registration Form

5. Write e **and** c.

t _e_ ach _e_ r   t ___ ach ___ r   t ___ ach ___ r

stud _e_ nt   stud ___ nt   stud ___ nt

_c_ ountry   ___ ountry   ___ ountry

**6. Work with a partner. Complete the form.
Ask each other questions.**

STUDENT : _____

COUNTRY : _____

TEACHER : _____   LEVEL: _____

CITY ADULT SCHOOL

Registration Form

**7. Work with a partner. Ask the questions.
Write the answers.**

➤ What country are you from?

● _____

➤ Who's your teacher?

● _____

1. Listen and practice the dialog.

- What room is Mr. Klein's class in?
➤ Room 30.
- Room 30?
➤ That's right.
- And where's the men's room?
➤ Next to room 30.
- Thanks.

2. Which is your bathroom? Circle the letter.

a.   b.

3. Listen. Circle the word you hear.

a. (Men's Room)   Women's Room   Office

b. Men's Room   Women's Room   Office

c. Men's Room   Women's Room   Office

4. Say the letters. Write the letters.

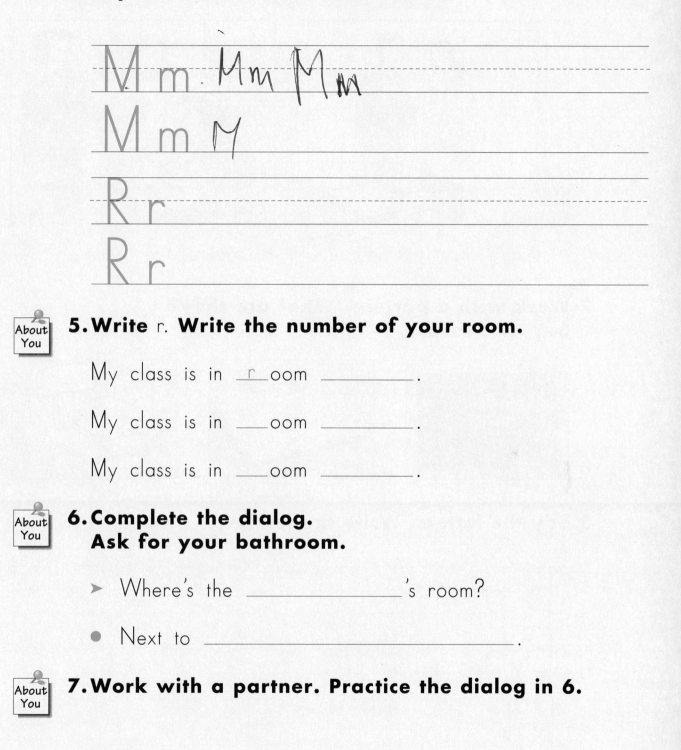

M m Mm Mm

M m M

R r

R r

5. Write r. **Write the number of your room.**

My class is in __r__ oom _____.

My class is in ____oom _____.

My class is in ____oom _____.

6. Complete the dialog.
   Ask for your bathroom.

➤ Where's the _____'s room?

● Next to _____.

7. Work with a partner. Practice the dialog in 6.

Board   Book   Desk

1. Listen and practice.

➤ Please sit at this desk.   ➤ Look at the board.

2. Work with a partner. What are they?
Say the words.

3. Say the letters. Write the letters.

B b

B b

K k

K k

4. Write b **and** k.

<u>b</u>oard   ___oard   ___oard   ___oard

des<u> k </u>   des___   des___   des___

<u>b</u> oo <u>k</u>   ___oo___   ___oo___   ___oo___

5. Listen. Circle the number.

a.

1.

2.

b.

1.

2.

6. Work with a partner.
Circle the board, book, and desk.
Underline the student and teacher.

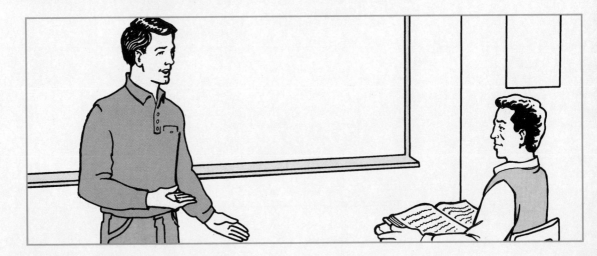

◆ Put It Together

1. Look at the map of a school.
Find the office, men's room, and women's room.

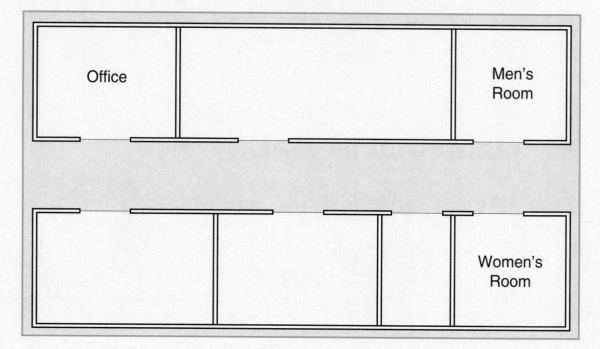

2. Work with a partner. Draw a map of your school.
Write your room number. Write where the
men's room, women's room, **and** office **are.**

I. Circle the word.

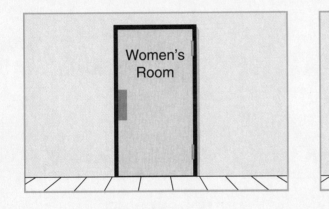

(teacher)

student

desk

book

student

teacher

desk

book

2. Which is your bathroom? Circle the letter.

a.

b.

3. Write the answers.

➤ What room is your class in?

● Room _____.

➤ Who's your teacher?

● _____

➤ What country are you from?

● _____

Write the words.

1. fficoe

o _f_ _f_ i _c_ e

2. skde

de _____ _____ _____

3. kobo

_____ oo _____

4. eatchre

tea _____ h _____ r

5. tsdentu

_____ tude _____ t

6. lbriary

l _____ br _____ ry

Look at the picture.

Where are the people?

What are they doing?

Time

1. Listen and practice the dialog.

> ➤ What time is it?
> ● It's 7:30.
> ➤ Excuse me?
> ● 7:30.
> ➤ Thanks.

2. Say the time.

a. It's 4:00.

b. It's 5:15.

c. It's 12:45.

d. It's 10:20.

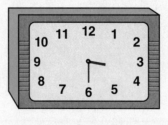

e. It's 3:30.

f. It's 7:50.

3. Listen. Circle the times you hear.

a. 7:00 (7:30) 6:00   **b.** 9:00   9:30   1:00

c. 3:00   2:00   3:30   **d.** 6:00   7:00   7:30

4. Circle the times.

TIME CARD

Employee Name: *Janice Watson*
Employee Number: *109*

TIME IN	TIME OUT
(8:29)	5:25
8:15	5:30
8:25	5:15

5. Write the times.

a. ___7:25___   **b.** _____   **c.** _____

**6. Talk to a partner.
Ask and say the time.**

7. Ask your partner the time.

Days of the Week

I. Listen and practice the dialog.

Fall Class Schedule						
	MON.	TUES.	WED.	THURS.	FRI.	SAT.
ESL 1		10:00		10:00		
ESL 2	11:00		11:00			
ESL 3						9:00
ESL 4			1:00			

➤ When is your English class?
● My class is on Monday and Wednesday.
 How about you?
➤ My class is on Tuesday and Thursday.

2. Say the letters. Write the letters.

D d

D d

W w

W w

Y y

Y y

3. **Write** W **and** y. **Say the words.**

<u>W</u>ednesda<u>y</u>   ___ednesda___   ___ednesda___

Write d **and** y. **Say the words.**

Mon<u>d</u>a<u>y</u>   Mon___a___   Thurs___a___

Satur___a___   Satur___a___   Sun___a___

4. **Circle the days and times of English 1.**

VILLAGE **ADULT** LEARNING CENTER SCHEDULE		Monday	Tuesday	Wednesday	Thursday	Friday
	English 1	7:30		7:30		
	English 2		8:00		8:00	
	English 3		7:15	7:15		

5. **Listen. Circle the days you hear.**

a. Monday   (Tuesday)   Wednesday

b. Tuesday   Wednesday   Thursday

c. Saturday   Sunday   Monday

d. Saturday   Thursday   Friday

About You

6. **Work with a partner.**
Make a schedule of your English class.

Class	Mon.	Tues.	Wed.	Thurs.	Fri.	Sat.

1. Listen and practice the dialog.

May						
S	**M**	**T**	**W**	**T**	**F**	**S**
	1	2	3	4	5	6
7	8	9	10	11	12	13
14	15	16	17	18	19	20
21	22	23	24	25	26	27
28	29	30	31			

➤ What's today's date?
● May 14.
➤ Oh, no. Tomorrow is my sister's birthday.

2. Your teacher says the numbers. You say the numbers.

1st	20th	30th
2nd	21st	31st
3rd	22nd	
4th	23rd	
	24th	

3. Listen. Circle the date you hear.

a.	July 1	July 2	(July 3)	July 4
b.	June 9	June 10	June 11	June 12
c.	October 11	October 12	October 13	October 15
d.	July 5	July 15	July 17	July 19

4. Write the dates.

			March			
S	**M**	**T**	**W**	**T**	**F**	**S**
	1	2	3	4	5	6
7	8	9	10	11	12	13
14	(15)	16	17	18	19	20
21	22	23	24	25	26	27
28	29	30	31			

			August			
S	**M**	**T**	**W**	**T**	**F**	**S**
1	2	3	4	5	6	7
(8)	9	10	11	12	13	14
15	16	17	18	19	20	21
22	23	24	25	26	27	28
29	30	31				

			September			
S	**M**	**T**	**W**	**T**	**F**	**S**
		1	2	3	4
5	6	(7)	8	9	10	11
12	13	14	15	16	17	18
19	20	21	22	23	24	25
26	27	28	29	30		

a. <u>March 15</u>   **b.** _____   **c.** _____

5. Work with a partner. Circle the dates. Say the dates.

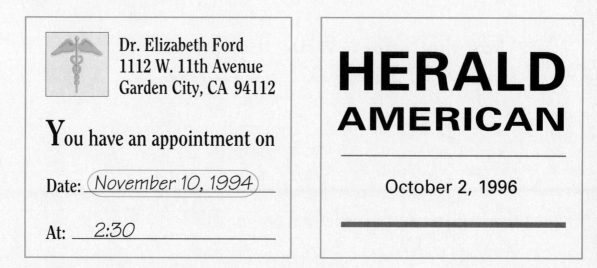

Dr. Elizabeth Ford
1112 W. 11th Avenue
Garden City, CA 94112

You have an appointment on

Date: (November 10, 1994)

At: 2:30

HERALD
AMERICAN

October 2, 1996

About You

6. Work with a partner. Ask the questions. Write the answers.

➤ What's today's date?

● _____

➤ What's tomorrow's date?

● _____

Date of Birth   Month   Year

1. Listen and practice the dialog.

January	February	March
April	May	June
July	August	September
October	November	December

➤ What's your date of birth?
● July 3, 1968.
➤ Excuse me? What year?
● 1968.

2. Say the letters. Write the letters.

J j

J j

U u

U u

V v

V v

3. Write J and u. Say the words.

J u ne _____ ne _____ ne _____ ne

J u ly _____ ly _____ ly _____ ly

Write v. Say the word.

No v ember   No___ember   No___ember

No___ember   No___ember   No___ember

4. Look at Ellen's date of birth.

Date of birth: _____March 17, 1966_____

Write your date of birth: _____

About You

5. Talk to other students. Complete the chart.

BIRTHDAYS

Name	Month	Day
Maria	March	2

Put It Together

1. Make a schedule for the week.
Write the days and times you go to school.
Write the days and times you go to work.

Sunday	
Monday	
Tuesday	
Wednesday	
Thursday	
Friday	
Saturday	

2. Write. Answer the questions.

a. When do you go to school?

b. When do you go to work?

Check Your Competency

1. Write the times.

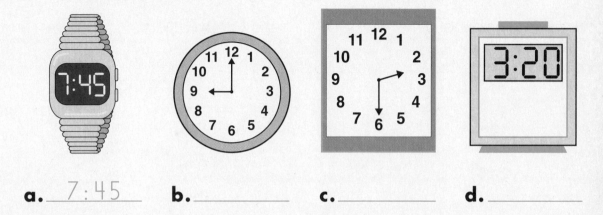

a. <u>7:45</u>   b. _____   c. _____   d. _____

2. Circle the days. Underline the months.

(Friday)	<u>May</u>	Wednesday
October	Tuesday	August
Sunday	December	March
January	Saturday	Monday
Thursday	September	April

3. Write the dates.

| **April 1993** |
| S M T W T F S |
| 1 2 |
| 3 4 5 6 7 8 9 |
| 10 11 12 13 14 (15) 16 |
| 17 18 19 20 21 22 23 |
| 24 25 26 27 28 29 30 |

| **November 1997** |
| S M T W T F S |
| 1 |
| 2 3 4 5 6 7 8 |
| 9 10 11 12 (13) 14 15 |
| 16 17 18 19 20 21 22 |
| 23 24 25 26 27 28 29 |
| 30 |

| **January 1985** |
| S M T W T F S |
| 1 (2) |
| 3 4 5 6 7 8 9 |
| 10 11 12 13 14 15 16 |
| 17 18 19 20 21 22 23 |
| 24 25 26 27 28 29 30 |
| 31 |

a. <u>April 15, 1993</u>   b. _____   c. _____

4. Write your date of birth.

_____

Extension

1. Work with a partner. Write the months in order.

February	January
December	__________
March	__________
May	__________
November	__________
June	__________
July	__________
September	__________
April	__________
January	__________
August	__________
October	__________

Unit 5 Food

Look at the picture.

Where are the people?

What are they doing?

61

Food

a. apples   b. bananas   c. oranges   d. onions

e. tomatoes   f. potatoes   g. milk

h. eggs   i. chicken   j. ground beef

k. rice   l. bread   m. cereal

1. Listen and practice the dialog.

➤ What do you want?
● Apples.

2. Circle the word.

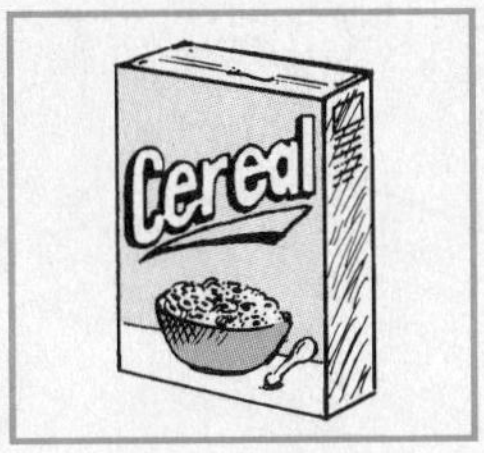

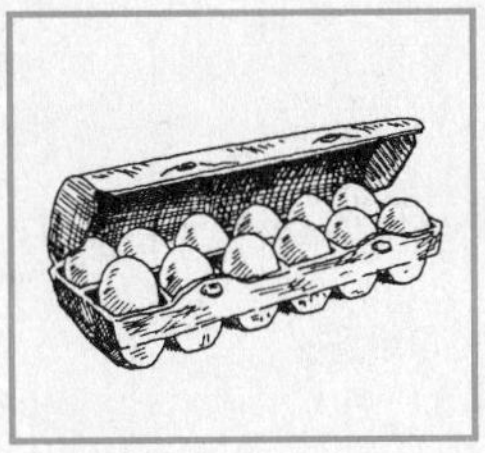

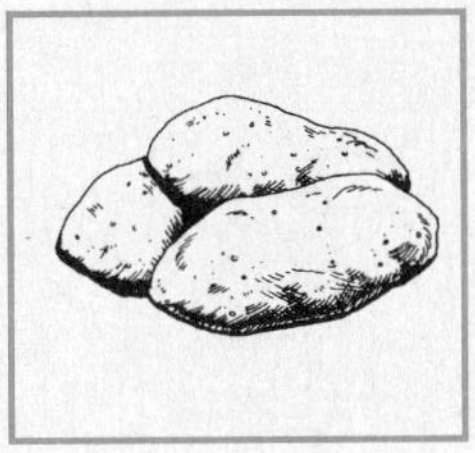

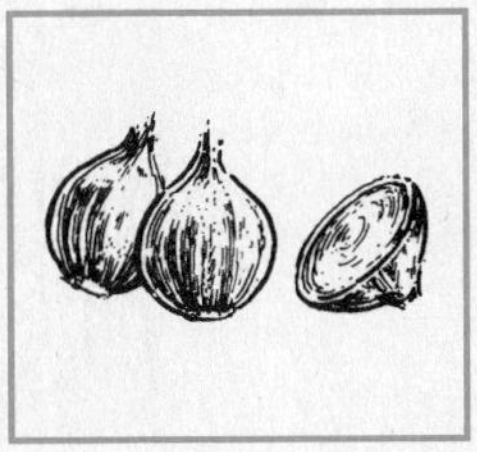

cereal
milk

tomatoes
eggs

oranges
potatoes

onions
apples

3. Listen. Circle the number of the food you hear.

a. 1.   2.

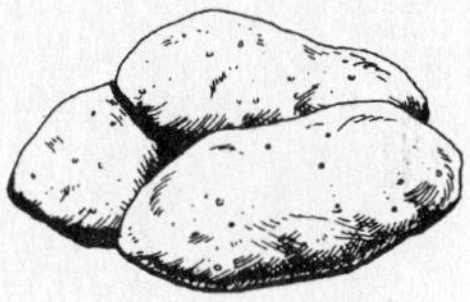

b. 1. 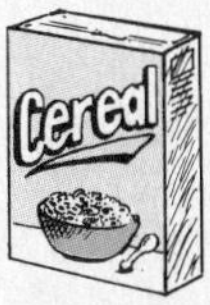   2.

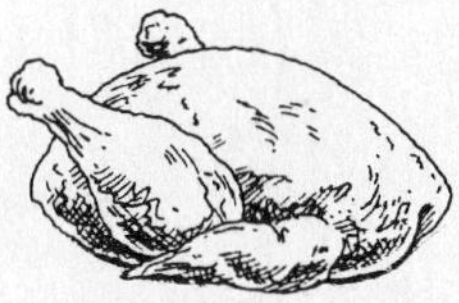

c. 1. 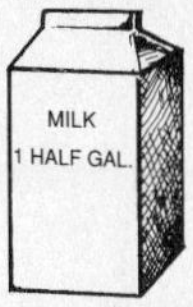   2.

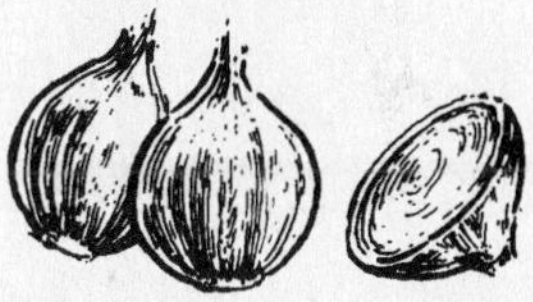

4. Work with a partner.
Write the number of the food.

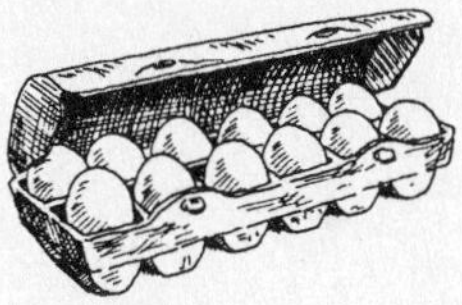

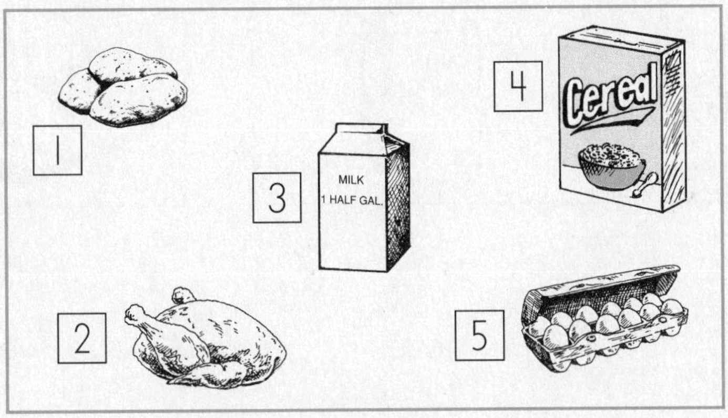

About You

1		
3	4	
2	5	

2 chicken

cereal

potatoes

milk

eggs

1. Listen and practice the dialogs.

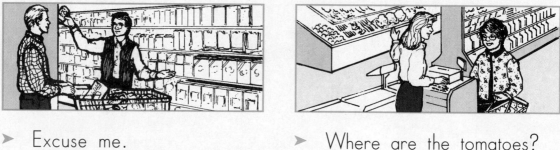

➤ Excuse me.
　Where's the chicken?
● In the meat section.

➤ Where are the tomatoes?
● On aisle 1.
➤ Thanks.

2. Say the letters. Write the letters.

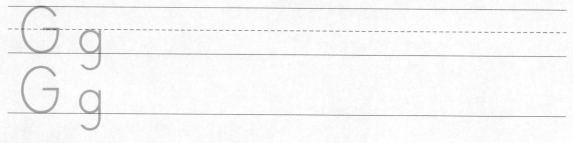

G g
G g

3. Write g. Say the words.

e_g_g　　　　e_____　　　　e_____

ve_g_etables　　ve___etables　　ve___etables

4. Circle the word.

dairy
(meat)

dairy
meat

meat
fruit and vegetables

5. Circle Meat, Fruit, **and** Dairy.

Meat
Fish
Poultry

Fresh
Fruit and
Vegetables

Dairy

6. Listen. Circle the aisle number you hear.

   a. Aisle 1   (Aisle 2)   Aisle 3

   b. Aisle 1   Aisle 2   Aisle 3

   c. Aisle 4   Aisle 5   Aisle 6

About You

7. Work with a partner. Complete the words. Write the letters.

Fruit and Vegetables	Dairy	Meat
_a_ p _p_ les	m __ lk	c __ ic __ e __
on __ o __ s	e __ g __	g __ ound b __ ef
p __ ta __ o __ s		

1. Listen and practice the dialog.

➤   What's left on the list?
●   A box of cereal, a bottle of juice, and a bag of rice.
➤   You get the cereal and rice. I'll get the juice.
●   OK.

2. Say the letters. Write the letters.

X x

X x

3. Write x. **Say the word.**

bo x   bo___   bo___   bo___   bo___

4. Circle box, bag, **or** bottle.

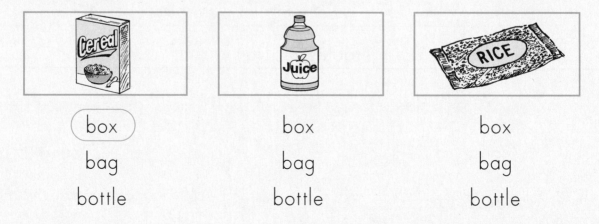

box   box   box

bag   bag   bag

bottle   bottle   bottle

5. Circle box, bag, **and** bottle.

Tissues $1.19 a (box)

Oranges $2.00 a bag

Water $3.00 for a 2-gallon bottle

6. Work with a partner. How do you buy the food? Check the box.

	Box	Bottle	Bag
Rice	☑	☐	☑
Cereal	☐	☐	☐
Juice	☐	☐	☐

7. Work with a partner. Look at the directions. What do you need? Write a list.

Quick Corn Muffin Mix

Ingredients:

2 eggs
1/2 cup milk

GROCERY LIST

_____

_____

_____

_____

I. Listen and practice the dialogs.

➤ Ground beef is on sale at Quality Supermarket.
● How much is it?
➤ It's $1.89 a pound.
● That's a good price.

➤ Rice is on sale at Z-Mart.
● How much is it?
➤ It's 79¢.
● That's a good price.

2. Say the letters. Write the letters.

Q q

Z z

Q q   Z z

3. Write Q and Z. Say the words.

Quality Supermarket   ___uality Supermarket

Z-Mart   ___-Mart   ___-Mart   ___-Mart

4. Write the amounts.

two dollars   <u> $2.00   </u>

twenty cents   <u>   </u>

seventy-nine cents   <u>   </u>

a dollar sixty-nine   <u>   </u>

5. Circle $, ¢, Sale, Supermarket, Eggs, Juice, Ground Beef, **and** Bread.

On Sale at **Quality Supermarket** This Week

Eggs **89¢** a carton

Bread **99¢** a loaf

Juice **$1⁹⁹** a bottle — Juice **$1²⁹** a bottle

Onions **50¢** a pound

Ground Beef **$1⁸⁹** a pound

Tomatoes **$1⁹⁹** a pound

6. Work with a partner. Look at 5. Write the price.

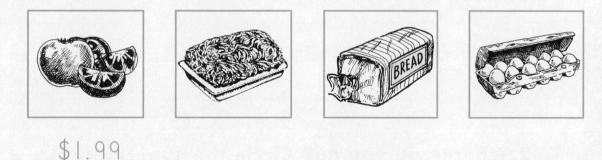

<u> $1.99 </u>   <u>   </u>   <u>   </u>   <u>   </u>

◆ Put It Together

1. Work with a partner. Look at the pictures. What do you want? Write a list.

Z-MART **This Week** SALE

Juice **$1⁵⁹** a bottle	Rice **79¢** a bag	Tomatoes **$1⁵⁰** a pound
Chicken **$1²⁹** a pound		Cereal **$2²⁹** a box
Eggs **79¢** a carton		

SALE **Quality Supermarket** SALE
THIS WEEK

Eggs **89¢** a carton	Bread **99¢** a loaf
Ground Beef **$1⁸⁹** a pound	
Juice **$1²⁹** a bottle	Onions **50¢** a pound
	Tomatoes **$1⁹⁹** a pound

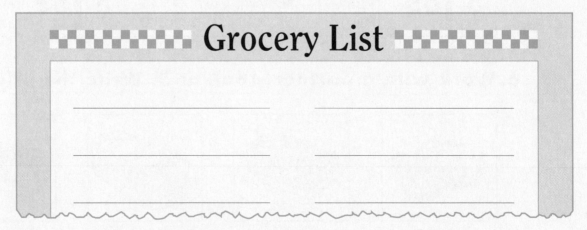

▪▪▪▪▪▪ Grocery List ▪▪▪▪▪▪

_____   _____

_____   _____

_____   _____

2. Where will you go? Circle the supermarket.

Quality Supermarket   Z-Mart

Check Your Competency

1. Circle the word.

rice
(bread)
juice

apples
potatoes
oranges

eggs
milk
ground beef

2. Circle box, bag, **or** bottle.

(box)
bag
bottle

box
bag
bottle

box
bag
bottle

3. Write the price.

milk _____ $1.09_____

bread _____

eggs _____

Complete the puzzle.

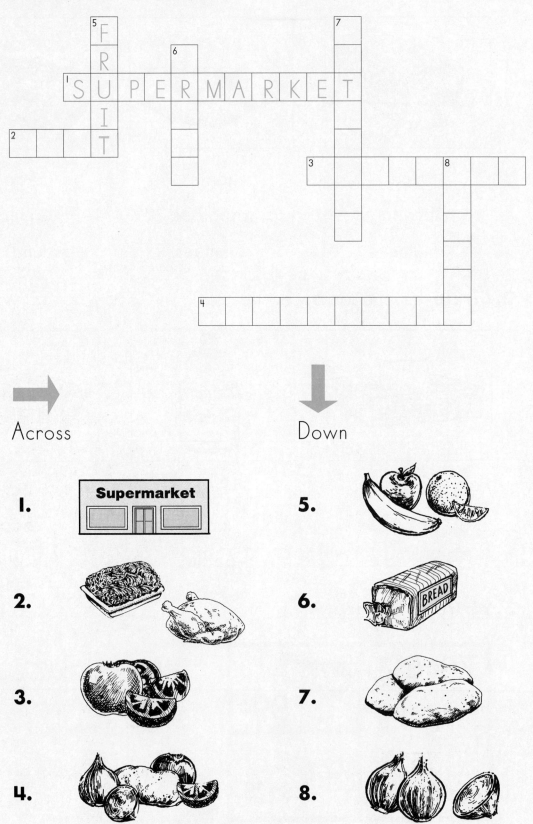

Across

1. Supermarket

2.

3.

4.

Down

5.

6.

7.

8.

Shopping

Look at the picture.

Where are the people?

What are they doing?

Cash   Charge

1. Listen and practice the dialogs.

➤ How much are these shoes?   ➤ How much is this shirt?
● They're $20.00.   ● It's $8.00.
➤ I'll take them.   ➤ I'll take it.
● Cash or charge?   ● Cash or charge?
➤ Charge.   ➤ Cash.

2. Say the names of the clothes.

a. sweater   **b.** coat   **c.** pants   **d.** socks

3. Say the words. Write the words.

cash   charge

4. Circle CASH and CHARGE.

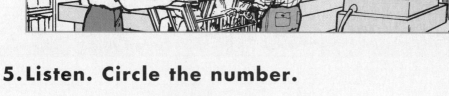

5. Listen. Circle the number.

a.
(1.)

2.

b.
1.

2.

c.
1.

2.

6. Work with a partner. Practice the dialog.
Talk about the clothes.

About You

SHIRT SIZE M
$20.00

PANTS SIZE L
$30.00

COAT SIZE S
$50.00

➤ How much is the shirt?
● It's $20.00.

1. Listen and practice the dialog.

➤ How much is the TV?
● It's $65.50.
➤ I'll take it.

2. Work with a partner. Say the names of the money.

a. a penny   **b.** a nickel   **c.** a dime   **d.** a quarter
one cent   five cents   ten cents   twenty-five cents

e. one dollar   **f.** five dollars   **g.** ten dollars   **h.** twenty dollars

About
You

3. Work with a partner. Say the amounts.
Write the amounts.

a. $2.00   **b.** _____   **c.** _____   **d.** _____

4. Circle NICKELS, DIMES, QUARTERS, **and** DOLLAR.

COLD DRINKS

$1.25

USE QUARTERS,
(NICKELS) DIMES,
OR DOLLAR BILLS.
NO PENNIES.

PeppO
DIET PeppO
Orange
Spritz

5. Listen. Circle the amount you hear.

a.	$21.98	($21.99)	$29.00
b.	$15.01	$15.10	$15.00
c.	85¢	$85.00	$8.50

6. Work with a partner. Practice the dialog. Talk about the items.

About You

$11.95

$1.25

$89.95

➤ How much is the shirt?
● It's $11.95.
➤ I'll take it.

1. Listen and practice the dialog.

➤ Cash, check, or charge?
● Check.
➤ OK. Please show me some ID.
● Here's my driver's license.

2. Work with a partner. Look at the check. Answer the questions.

Ana Soto   **581**
386 Ocean Avenue
Long Beach, CA   DATE *January 31, 1995*

PAY TO THE
ORDER OF *Northwest Hardware* $ *32.50*

Thirty-two and 50/100   DOLLARS

✳ **CAL**BANK   *Ana Soto*

a. How much is the check for? _____

b. What store is the check to? _____

3. Write the amounts for a check.

a. $15.95 Fifteen and 95/100 _____ DOLLARS

b. $21.50 _____ DOLLARS

c. $3.75 _____ DOLLARS

4. Circle CHECK, checks, ID, **and** driver's license.

STORE CHECK POLICY

1. No out-of-state checks.

2. Name and address on checks.

3. A driver's license or another form of ID.

5. Write a check to Northwest Hardware for $34.78.

	226
DATE _____	
PAY TO THE ORDER OF _____	$ [ ]
_____ DOLLARS	
✳ **CAL**BANK	_____

Receipt

> ➤ I want to return this chair.
> ● Give me the receipt, please.
> ➤ Here.

2. Answer the questions.

a. What is he returning? _____

b. Does he have the receipt? _____

3. Look at the receipts. Circle the totals.

SHOP 'N SAVE MARKETS
8040 MESA DRIVE

LARGE ORANGES	$ .10
APPLES	.69
JUICE	1.35
MILK	1.35
BREAD	1.29
TOTAL	$4.78

24-HOUR DELI

MILK	$1.25
SANDWICH	4.00
TOTAL	$5.25

4. Match the receipt and the money.

Quality Mart

Bread	$ 1.20
Meat	1.90
Fish	6.52
Juice	1.78
Total	$11.40

Thank You For Shopping
at McClane's

Aspirin	$ 4.23
Sunglasses	$ 5.77
Total	$10.00

July 15, 1994
DART DISCOUNT STORE

Shirt	$10.00
Socks	6.00
TOTAL	$16.00

Thanks for shopping at DART!

SHOETOWN
06/02/95

Shoes	$26.00
Total	$26.00
Cash	$26.00
Change	$00.00

◆ Put It Together

Look at the picture. What do you want?
Buy it. Complete the check.

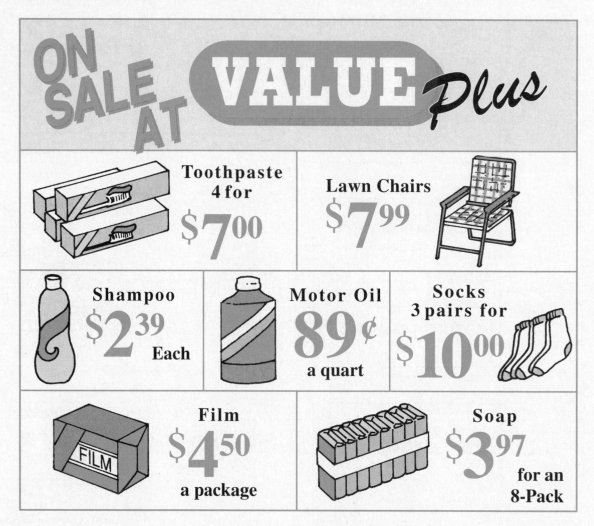

ON SALE AT **VALUE** *Plus*

Toothpaste
4 for
$7⁰⁰

Lawn Chairs
$7⁹⁹

Shampoo
$2³⁹ Each

Motor Oil
89¢
a quart

Socks
3 pairs for
$10⁰⁰

Film
$4⁵⁰
a package

Soap
$3⁹⁷
for an
8-Pack

227

DATE _____

PAY TO THE
ORDER OF _____ $ [ ]

_____ DOLLARS

✳ **CAL**BANK   _____

Check Your Competency

1. Circle the word.

a. (shoes)
pants

b. socks
shoes

c. shirt
coat

d. shirt
sweater

2. Write the amounts.

a. _____39¢_____

b. _____

c. _____

3. Look at the receipt. Complete the check.

McClane's Drug Store
Prescription $21.50
Aspirin   6.20
        Total $27.70

228

DATE _____

PAY TO THE
ORDER OF _____ $ [   ]

_____ DOLLARS

✳ CALBANK   _____

Circle the words.

✔ CASH
CHECK
RECEIPT
CHARGE
DOLLAR
CENTS

```
B  T  C  O  R  H  K  S
Z  L  N  Y  C  A  S  H
K  C  H  E  C  K  W  L
I  D  R  J  Q  B  E  S
Y  R  E  C  E  I  P  T
P  C  H  A  R  G  E  N
V  T  O  S  K  C  W  L
S  Y  D  O  L  L  A  R
L  Q  H  A  V  W  S  I
P  C  E  N  T  S  C  J
```

Home

Look at the picture.

Where are the people?

What are they doing?

House   Apartment

1. Listen and practice the dialog.

➤ What's your address?

● 704 Main Steet.

➤ Is it a house or an apartment?

● An apartment.

2. Write apartment **or** house.

a. <u>apartment</u>   **b.** _____   **c.** _____

3. Listen. Circle the answer.

a. Manuel lives in   (an apartment.)   a house.

b. Sandra lives in   an apartment.   a house.

c. Mike lives in   an apartment.   a house.

4. Circle house **and** apartment.

5. Write your address. Write a house **or** an apartment.

a. My address is _____.

b. I live in _____.

6. Write the sentences in 5.

_____

_____

7. Work with a group. Complete the chart.

NAME	HOUSE	APARTMENT
Anna	✔	

1. Listen and practice the dialog.

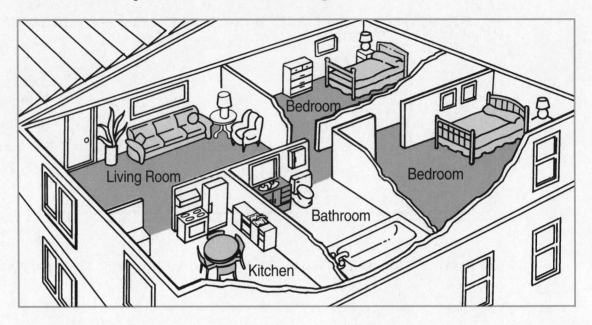

> ➤ This apartment is nice.
> ● Yes, it is. It has two bedrooms, a bathroom, a living room, and a big kitchen.

2. Circle the room.

a. (kitchen)   **b.** bathroom   **c.** living room   **d.** bathroom

living room   bedroom   bathroom   bedroom

3. Listen. Circle the room you hear.

a. bathroom   (bedroom)

b. kitchen   bedroom

c. living room   bathroom

4. Circle Kitchen, Bedroom, Bathroom, **and** Living Room.

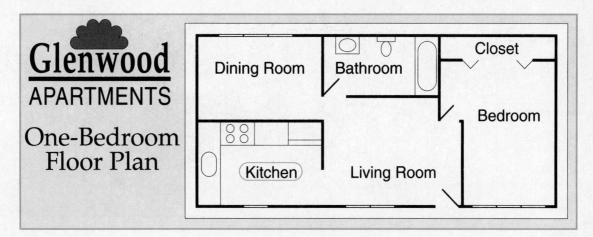

5. Say the words. Write the words.

kitchen   bedroom   bathroom

_____   _____   _____

_____   _____   _____

_____   _____   _____

About You

6. Work with a partner.
Write the rooms in your house or apartment.
Write the rooms in your partner's house
or apartment.

My House	My Partner's House
_____	_____
_____	_____
_____	_____
_____	_____

1. Listen and practice the dialog.

> ➤ Is the apartment furnished?
> ● Yes. There's a bed, a sofa, and a chair.
> ➤ What's in the kitchen?
> ● A table, a refrigerator, and a stove.
> ➤ Are there any lamps?
> ● Yes. There are two lamps.

2. Work with a partner. Say the words.

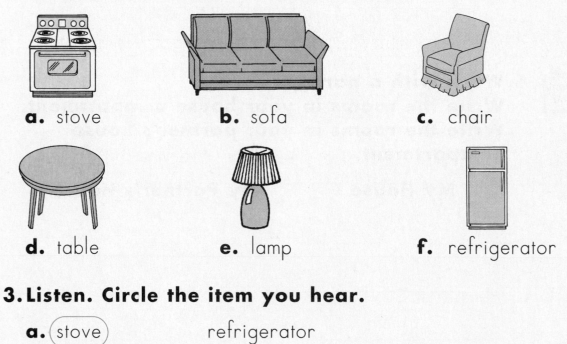

a. stove   **b.** sofa   **c.** chair

d. table   **e.** lamp   **f.** refrigerator

3. Listen. Circle the item you hear.

a. (stove)   refrigerator

b. sofa   chair

c. refrigerator   lamp

4. Circle Lamps, Stoves, Sofas, Chairs, Tables, Beds, **and** Refrigerators.

5. Work with a partner. Write the words.

<u>stove</u>   _____   _____   _____

_____   _____   _____   _____

6. Look at the ad in 4. What do you want to buy? Make a list. Write the prices.

Item	Price
Lamp	$19.99

Rent   Deposit

 I. Listen and practice the dialog.

➤ I need an apartment.
● There's a nice apartment in this building.
➤ How much is the rent?
● $350 a month.
➤ Is there a deposit?
● Yes. It's $300.

 2. Complete the sentences.

a. My rent is _____.

b. My deposit is _____.

 3. Write the sentences in 2.

_____

_____

4.Circle Apartments, apartment, Rent, **and** Deposit.

FOR RENT

1 Bedroom apartment

Rent: $425.00 a month

Deposit: $175

Call owner: 555-7980

Apartments For Rent

1 bedroom apartment
$250 a month plus electric
On bus route

Deposit $100
No pets

Call 343-8227
Available May 1

5.Listen. Circle rent **or** deposit.

a. (rent)   deposit

b. rent   deposit

c. rent   deposit

**6.Work with a partner. Read the ad.
Write the numbers.**

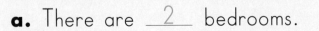

CLASSIFIED • RENTALS

Apartments For Rent

2 bedrooms. Rent $375 a month.
$100 deposit. Available July 1.
Call 555-3468

a. There are __2__ bedrooms.

b. The rent is _____.

c. The deposit is _____.

◆ Put It Together

What furniture do you have?
Write the furniture under the room.

| bed   sofa   chair   lamp   refrigerator   stove   table |

Living Room	Bedroom	Bathroom	Kitchen
	bed		

Check Your Competency

1. Write the correct word.

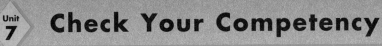

| table | sofa | lamp |

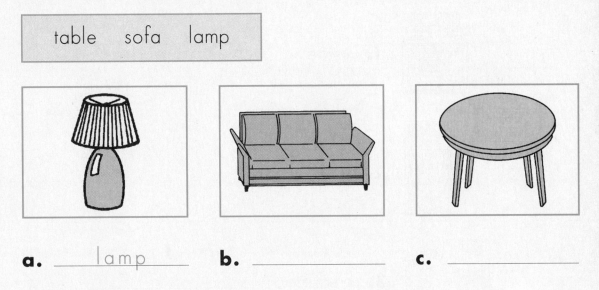

a. __lamp__   b. _____   c. _____

2. What room is it in? Write the room.

| bedroom | kitchen | living room |

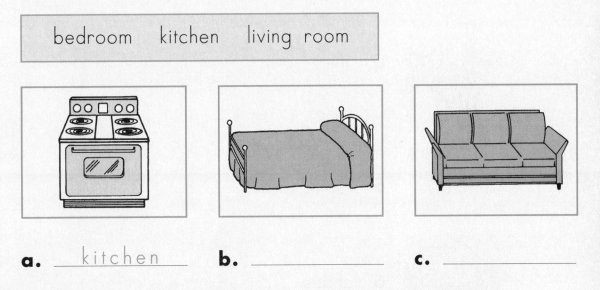

a. __kitchen__   b. _____   c. _____

3. Look at the newspaper ad. Write the numbers.

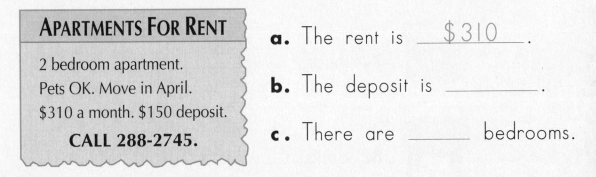

APARTMENTS FOR RENT

2 bedroom apartment.
Pets OK. Move in April.
$310 a month. $150 deposit.
CALL 288-2745.

a. The rent is __$310__.

b. The deposit is _____.

c. There are _____ bedrooms.

Extension

Unscramble the words.

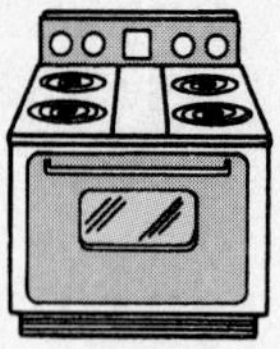

1. vstoe stove

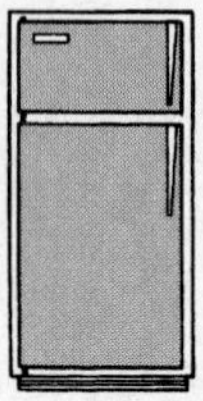

2. fritroergare ______________________

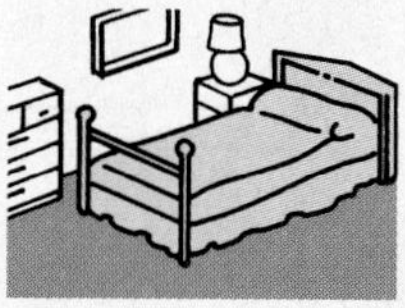

3. rmdeboo ______________

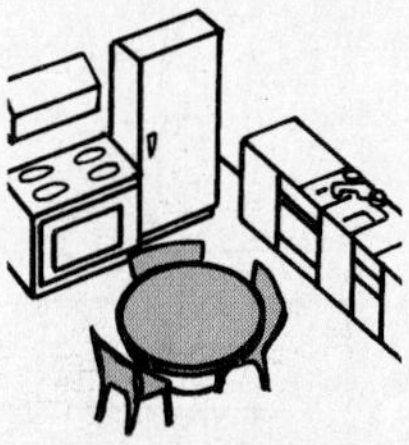

4. tchikne ______________

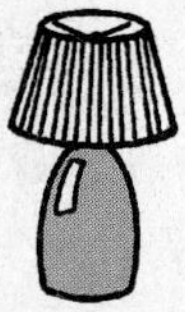

5. mpla __________

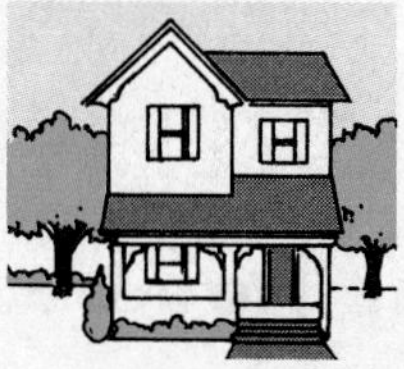

6. shoue ___________

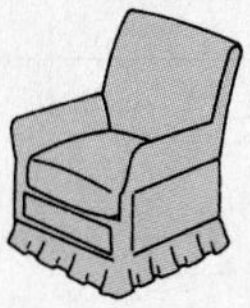

7. ihcar ___________

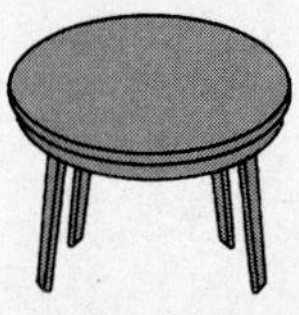

8. betla ___________

Health Care

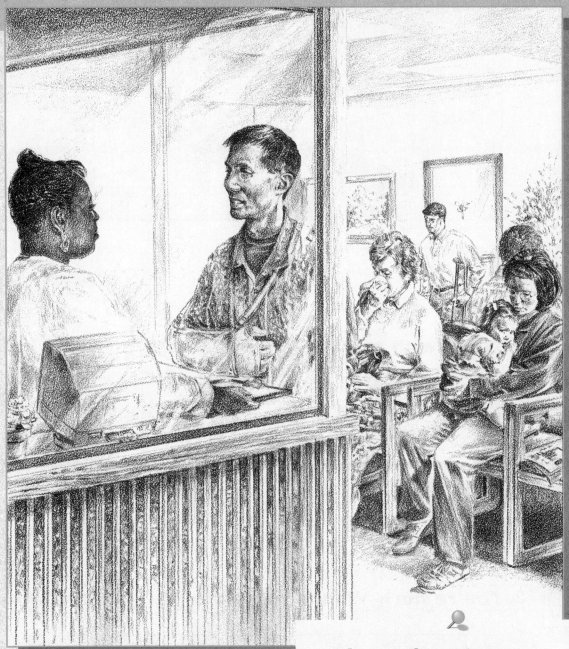

Look at the picture.

Where are the people?

What are they doing?

1. Listen and practice the dialog.

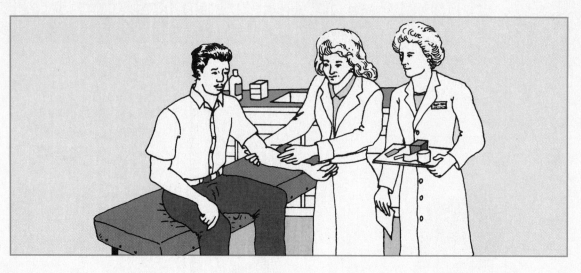

➤ What's the matter?
● My arm is hurt.
➤ OK. Let's check it.

2. Work with a partner. Say the sentences.

a. Her hand is cut.   **b.** His foot is hurt.   **c.** Her leg is broken.

About You 3. You're hurt. What's the matter? Circle the words.

My | arm hand foot leg | is | cut hurt broken | .

About You 4. Write the sentence in 3.

_____

5. Write the words.

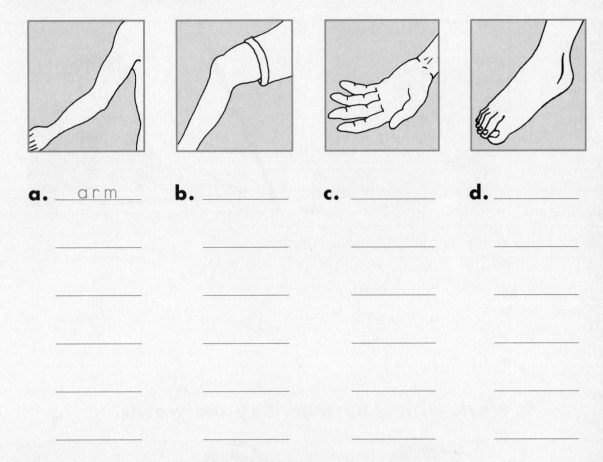

a. _arm_   **b.** _____   **c.** _____   **d.** _____

6. Listen. Circle the word you hear.

a. (arm)   leg

b. hand   foot

c. arm   foot

 ## 7. What's the matter? Complete the dialog.

➤ What's the matter?

● _____

 ## 8. Work with a partner. Practice the dialog in 7.

1. Listen and practice the dialog.

> ➤ Hello. Dr. Kendell's office.
> ● I'm sick. I want to see the doctor.
> ➤ What's the matter?
> ● I have a fever and a cough.
> ➤ Can you come in at 2:30?
> ● OK.

2. Work with a partner. Say the words.

a. fever   **b.** cough   **c.** sore throat

3. You're sick. What's the matter? Circle the word.

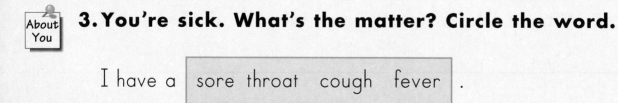

I have a | sore throat   cough   fever | .

4. Write the sentence in 3.

_____

5. Write the words.

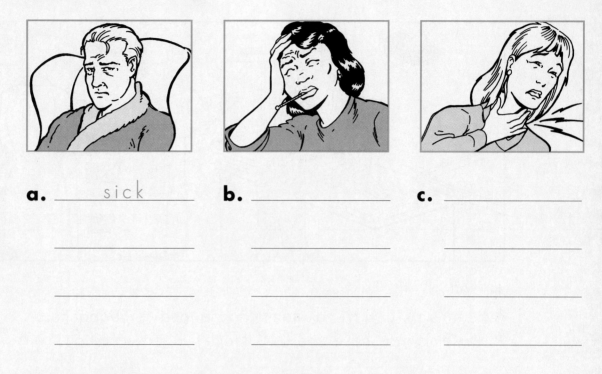

a. ___sick___   b. _____   c. _____

_____   _____   _____

_____   _____   _____

6. Listen. When will the people see the doctor? Circle the answers.

a. Tuesday at 8:30   (Tuesday at 10:30)

b. Wednesday at 10:00   Thursday at 10:00

c. Thursday at 4:45   Monday at 4:45

7. You want to see the doctor. Complete the dialog.

➤ I want to see the doctor.

● What's the matter?

➤ _____

8. Work with a partner. Practice the dialog in 7.

1. Listen and practice the dialog.

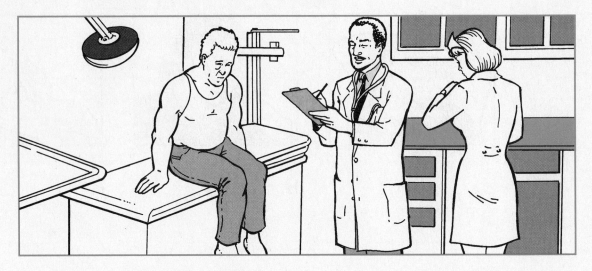

> ➤ What's the matter?
> ● I'm sick. I have a stomachache and a headache.
> ➤ I think you have the flu. Here's a prescription.

2. Work with a partner. Say the words.

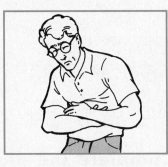  

a. stomachache   **b.** cold   **c.** headache

About You

3. You're sick. What's the matter? Circle the word.

I have a | stomachache cold headache |.

About You

4. Write the sentence in 3.

5. Write the words.

a. ___cold___   b. _____   c. _____

_____   _____   _____

_____   _____   _____

_____   _____   _____

6. Listen. What's the matter? Circle the answers.

a. headache   stomachache   (sore throat)

b. sore throat   headache   stomachache

c. headache   stomachache   sore throat

7. You're sick. Complete the dialog.

➤ I'm sick.

● What's the matter?

➤ I have a _____ .

8. Work with a partner. Practice the dialog in 7.

Medicine Tablet Capsule

1. Listen and practice the dialog.

➤ Take two tablets every four hours.

● OK.

2. Work with a partner. Say the words.

 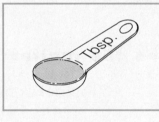 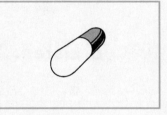

a. teaspoon **b.** tablespoon **c.** capsule

3. Listen. How much medicine do they take? Check the box.

	2 capsules	2 tablets	2 teaspoons	2 tablespoons
a.	✔			
b.				
c.				
d.				

4. Match.

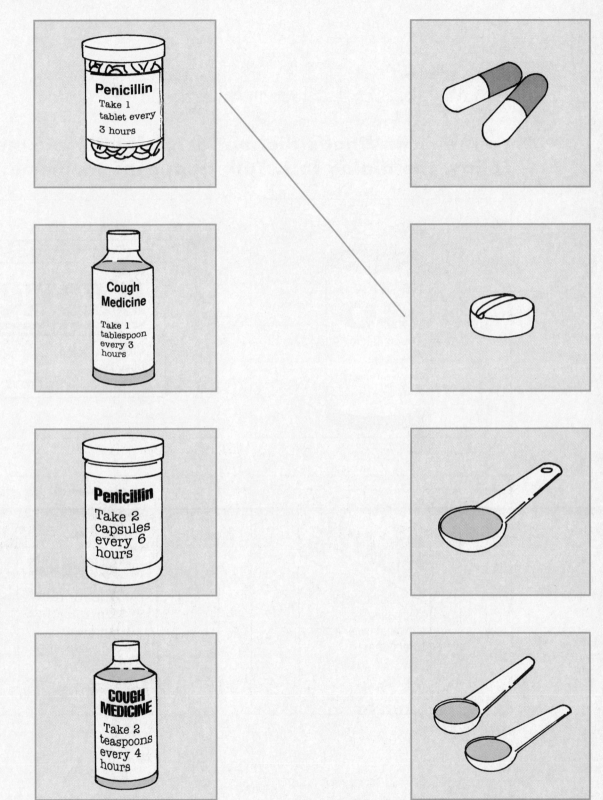

◆ Put It Together

1. Work with a partner. Practice the dialog.

➤ I'm sick. I have a headache.
● Take Nutrin.
➤ How much?
● Take two capsules, four times a day.

2. You're sick. What's the matter? Tell your partner. Follow the dialog in 1. Talk about the medicine.

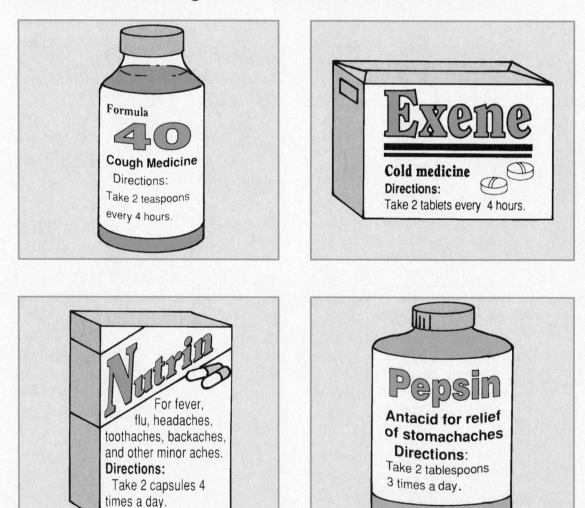

1. Write the correct word.

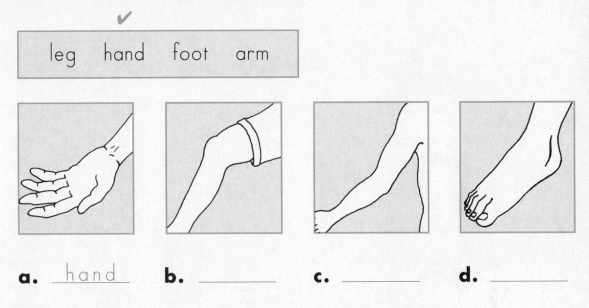

| leg | hand | foot | arm |

a. <u>hand</u>　　b. _____　　c. _____　　d. _____

2. What's the matter with each person?

| broken | headache |

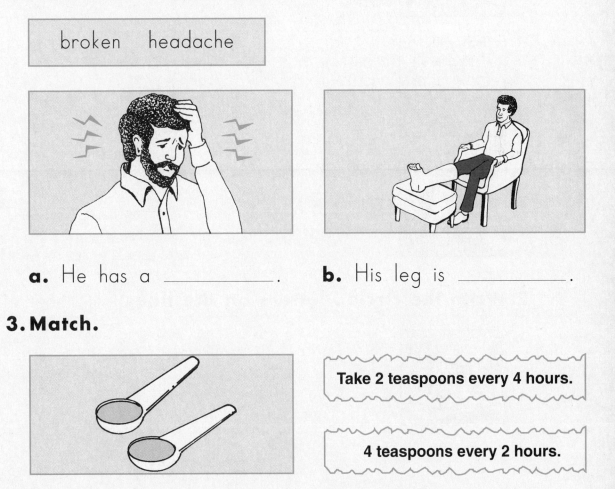

a. He has a _____ .　　b. His leg is _____ .

3. Match.

Take 2 teaspoons every 4 hours.

4 teaspoons every 2 hours.

1. Write the word for each picture.

H E A D (A) A C H E

_ _ (O) _ _

(O) _ _ _ _

_ _ _ _ (O) _ _ (O) _ _

_ _ _ (O) _

2. Write the circled letters on the lines.

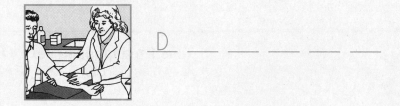

D _ _ _ _ _

9 Employment

Look at the picture.
Where are the people?
What are they doing?

Job

1. Listen and practice the dialog.

> ➤ I want a job.
> ● What do you do?
> ➤ I'm a cook.

2. Work with a partner. Say the names of the jobs.

a. painter

b. custodian

c. cook

d. clerk

e. mechanic

f. housekeeper

3. Listen. Circle the job you hear.

a. custodian   (cook)

b. painter   clerk

c. mechanic   housekeeper

4. Circle PAINTER, CUSTODIAN, HOUSEKEEPER, **and** MECHANIC.

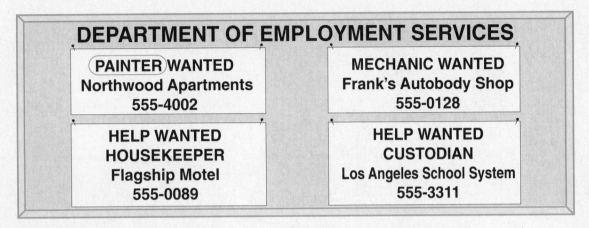

DEPARTMENT OF EMPLOYMENT SERVICES

(PAINTER) WANTED
Northwood Apartments
555-4002

MECHANIC WANTED
Frank's Autobody Shop
555-0128

HELP WANTED
HOUSEKEEPER
Flagship Motel
555-0089

HELP WANTED
CUSTODIAN
Los Angeles School System
555-3311

5. Write the job.

a. mechanic   b. _____   c. _____

_____   _____   _____

_____   _____   _____

_____   _____   _____

About You

6. Complete the sentence.

➤ What do you do?

● I'm a _____.

About You

7. Work with a partner. Practice the dialog in 6.

Application   Experience

 1. Listen and practice the dialog.

➤ I want to apply for the job.
● Do you have any experience?
➤ Yes, I do. I was a cook from 1991 to 1993.
● OK. Please complete this application.

 2. Complete the sentence.

I was a _____ from _____ to _____.

3. Write the sentence in 2.

_____

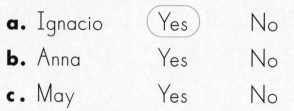 **4. Listen. Do they have any work experience?**
Circle Yes **or** No.

    a. Ignacio   (Yes)   No

    b. Anna   Yes   No

    c. May   Yes   No

5. Circle Experience **and** Application.

Job Application			
Name: *Li Chiu*			Telephone Number: *(712) 555-6321*
Address: *3701 Hart Lane, Apt. 21 Sacramento, CA 97521*			
Work (Experience)			
From	**To**	**Job**	**Employer**
1990	*1993*	*Housekeeper*	*Memorial Hospital*
1986	*1990*	*Clerk*	*Chan Exports*

6. Look at the application in 5. Answer the questions.

a. When was Li Chiu a housekeeper?

_____

b. Where was she a housekeeper?

_____

7. Complete the application.

Job Application			
Name:			Telephone Number:
Address:			
Work Experience			
From	**To**	**Job**	**Employer**

1. Listen and practice the dialog.

➤ Can you work nights?
● Yes, I can.
➤ Can you work weekends?
● No, I can't. I'm sorry.
➤ When can you start?
● Immediately.
➤ OK. Be here tomorrow night at 5:00.

2. Complete the sentences.
Write days, nights, **and** weekends.

I can work _____.

I can't work _____.

3. Write the sentences in 2.

_____

_____

4. Circle days, nights, **and** weekends.

Name: *Tom Fitzgerald*	Telephone Number: *(534) 555-3678*

Address: *645 Western Ave. San Francisco, CA 92342*

AVAILABILITY

Can you work weekends ?   (Yes)   No

Can you work (days) ?   (Yes)   No

Can you work nights ?   (Yes)   No

When can you start work?

Immediately   (In two weeks)   Other date: _____

5. Look at the application in 4. Circle the answers.

a. Can Tom work days?   (Yes)   No

b. Can Tom work weekends?   Yes   No

c. Can Tom work nights?   Yes   No

d. When can he start?   Immediately   In two weeks

About You

6. Complete the form.

AVAILABILITY

Can you work weekends?   Yes   No

Can you work days?   Yes   No

Can you work nights?   Yes   No

When can you start work?

Immediately   In two weeks   Other date: _____

1. Read the ads.

a.
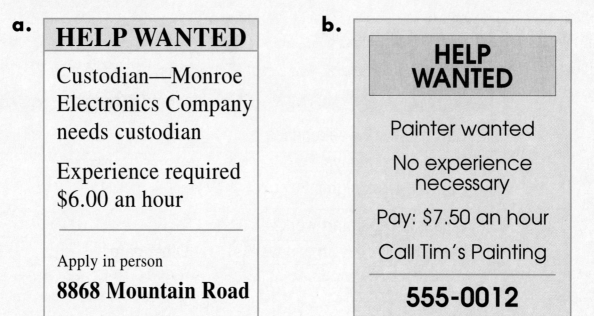

HELP WANTED

Custodian—Monroe Electronics Company needs custodian

Experience required
$6.00 an hour

_____

Apply in person

8868 Mountain Road

b.

HELP WANTED

Painter wanted

No experience necessary

Pay: $7.50 an hour

Call Tim's Painting

555-0012

2. Answer the questions. Write the letter of the ad.

a. The ad is for a custodian.   Ad _a_

b. No experience is required for this job.   Ad ____

c. The pay is $6.00 an hour for this job.   Ad ____

d. The ad is for a painter.   Ad ____

e. Experience is required for this job.   Ad ____

f. The pay is $7.50 an hour for this job.   Ad ____

About You

3. Write. Which job do you want?

Job applied for: _____

4. Circle Help Wanted, experience, **and** Experience.

Help Wanted

Cook Wanted.
Midnight Diner.
Experience required.
$5.00 an hour.
Weekends and nights.
37 Stuart Street.

Help Wanted

Housekeeper.
Hope Hospital.
No experience necessary.
Days.
$4.75 an hour.   Call 555-0301.

5. Look at the ads in 4. Which job do you want? Complete the application.

Job applied for: _____

◆ Put It Together

I. Look at the ads. Circle the job you want.

Mechanic needed—
Joe's Car Repair.
Full-time position.
$13.00 an hour.
Experience required.
Apply in person.
7 Unity Street.

Painter—
Dale's Painting Service.
Part-time position.
Experience preferred.
$9.00 an hour.
Call **555-2018.**

2. Complete the application.

JOB APPLICATION

Name:

Telephone Number:

Address:

Position Applied for:

WORK EXPERIENCE

From	To	Job	Employer

AVAILABILITY

Can you work days?	☐ Yes	☐ No
Can you work nights?	☐ Yes	☐ No
Can you work weekends?	☐ Yes	☐ No

When can you start work?

☐ Immediately   ☐ In two weeks

1. Answer the questions. Circle the ad.

a.

Mechanic Wanted
Marty's Garage.
$12 an hour.
Experience Required.

b.

Cook Wanted
Ray's Hamburgers.
Pay: $5.50 an hour.
No experience required.

1. The ad is for a mechanic.	(Ad a)	Ad b
2. The job pays $5.50 an hour.	Ad a	Ad b
3. Experience is required for this job.	Ad a	Ad b

2. Complete the application.

JOB APPLICATION

Name	Telephone Number
Address	
Position Applied for	

WORK EXPERIENCE

From	To	Job	Employer

AVAILABILITY

	Yes	No
Can you work days?	☐	☐
Can you work nights?	☐	☐
Can you work weekends?	☐	☐

When can you start work?

☐ Immediately   ☐ In two weeks

Complete the puzzle.

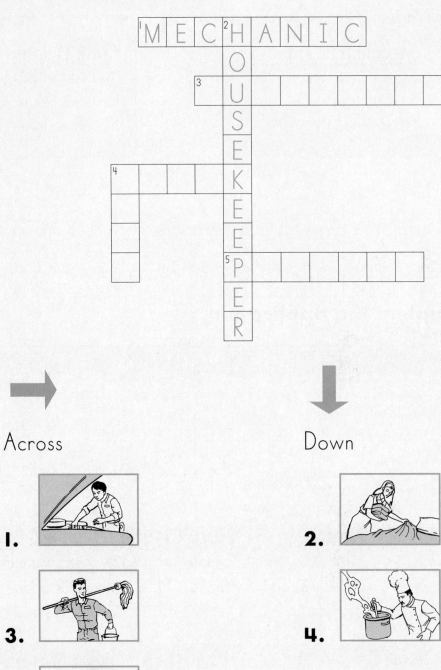

Across

Down

1.

2.

3.

4.

4.

5.

Look at the picture.

Where are the people?

What are they doing?

1. Listen and practice the dialog.

➤ How do you go to school?
● By bus.

2. Say the words.

| **a.** train | **b.** subway | **c.** car | **d.** bus | **e.** bicycle |

3. Listen. Circle the correct picture.

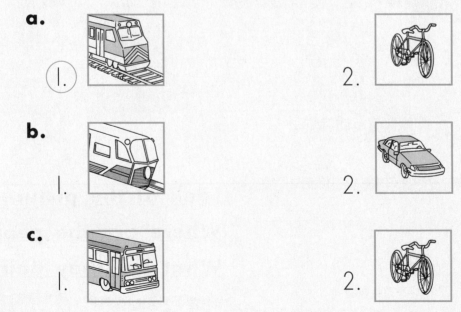

a.   1.   2.

b.   1.   2.

c.   1.   2.

4. Circle Bus, bus, Subway, subway, Car, **and** car.

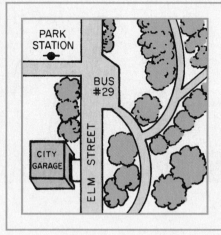

City Park, Fun for the Whole Family

You can get to the park by **car, subway , or city bus.**

Car –Take route 3 to Elm Street; park in the city garage.

Subway –Take a red line train to the Park subway stop.

City (Bus) –Take the #29 bus; get off at Elm Street.

5. Write the words.

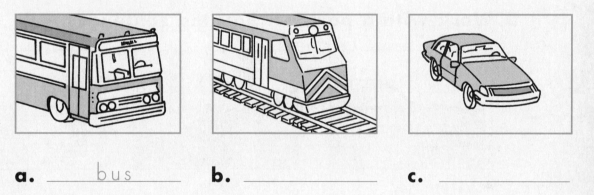

a. bus   **b.** _____   **c.** _____

_____   _____   _____

_____   _____   _____

About You

6. Write. Answer the questions.

a. How do you go to school? _____

b. How do you go to work? _____

c. How do you go to the supermarket? _____

d. How do you go to the bank? _____

Walk   Drive   Ride

1. Listen and practice the dialog.

> ➤ How do you go to school?
> ● I walk. How about you?
> ➤ I drive.

2. Work with a partner. Say the sentences.

a. She drives.   **b.** He walks.   **c.** He takes the bus.

d. She takes the train.   **e.** He rides his bicycle.

3. How do you go to school? Complete the sentence.

I _____ to school.

4. Write the sentence in 3.

_____

_____

5. Write. Answer the questions.

a. How do you go to school? _____

b. How do you go to the supermarket? _____

c. How do you go to the bank? _____

d. How do you go to work? _____

6. Work with a group. How do you go to school? Complete the chart.

NAME	CAR	BUS	WALK	SUBWAY	TRAIN	BICYCLE
Marion		✔				

1. Read the signs.

a. Don't walk

b. Walk

c. One way

d. Stop

e. Speed limit

f. No parking

2. Listen. Circle the correct sign.

a.

(1.)

2.

b.

1.

2.

c.

1.

2.

3. Circle STOP, WALK, ONE WAY, **and** SPEED LIMIT.

4. Look at the pictures. Circle the words.

 SPEED LIMIT 30   WALK

WALK   ONE WAY   SPEED LIMIT 30

5. Write the words.

a. _walk_   **b.** _____   **c.** _____

_____   _____   _____

_____   _____   _____

Bus Stop   Fare

1. Listen and practice the dialog.

> ➤ Does this bus go to Green Street?
> ● Yes, it does.
> ➤ How much is the fare?
> ● One dollar.

2. Where do the buses go? Match.

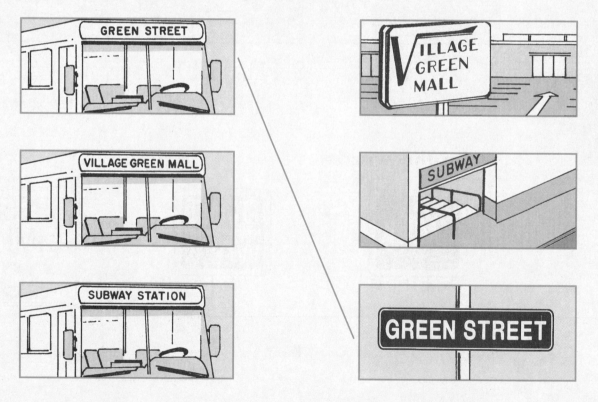

3. Work with a partner. You're at the bus stop. Ask for the buses in 2. Follow the dialog in 1.

4. Circle BUS STOP, Bus Stop, FARE, **and** Fare.

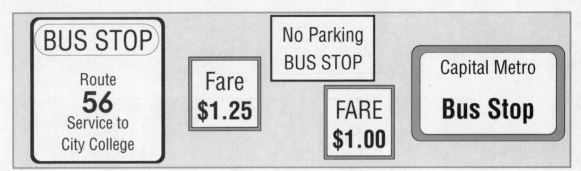

5. Listen. Where do the people want to go? Circle the place you hear.

a. (train station)   bus station

b. City Community College   Blue's Department Store

c. City Hall   Village Green Mall

d. City Hospital   Job Mart

Listen again. Write the fare.

a. $1.00

b. _____

c. _____

d. _____

6. Where do you want to go? Complete the dialog.

➤ Does this bus go to _____?

● Yes, it does.

7. Work with a partner. Practice the dialog in 6.

Work with a partner. Write the words on the picture.

bicycle   bus   car   subway   train

1. bicycle
2. _____
3. _____
4. _____
5. _____

DOWNTOWN

GREEN STREET

1. Write the word.

bus   train   car   bicycle

a. <u>bicycle</u>   **b.** _____   **c.** _____   **d.** _____

2. What do the signs say? Match.

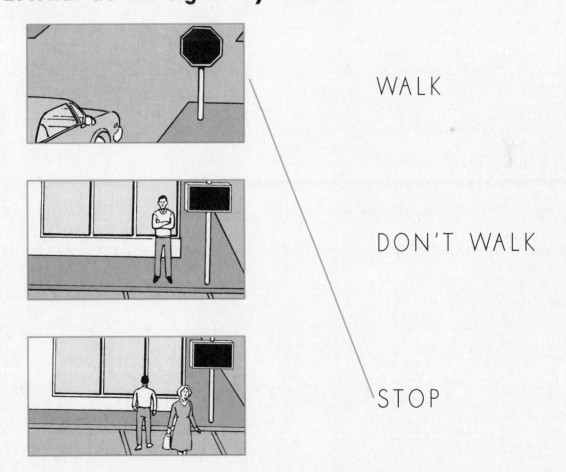

WALK

DON'T WALK

STOP

Extension

Circle the words.

✔ DRIVE
STOP
TRAIN
CAR
BICYCLE
WALK
BUS
SUBWAY

X	Y	Z	D	R	I	V	E	Y	Q
V	N	O	R	O	S	T	O	P	P
T	R	A	I	N	C	P	A	N	E
R	C	B	D	G	M	O	I	N	P
C	A	R	Q	Z	P	T	B	G	D
S	B	I	C	Y	C	L	E	A	I
A	L	L	W	A	L	K	W	L	A
S	Y	A	L	W	H	B	C	U	O
F	E	B	U	S	S	T	P	O	N
A	Y	A	Y	S	U	B	W	A	Y

Listening Transcript

Page 12
Exercise 3. Listen for *name*. Raise your hand.
a. A: What's your name?
   B: George Smith.
b. A: Who's that man?
   B: George Smith.
c. A: Who is she?
   B: Ellen Porch.
d. A: What do I do next?
   B: Please write your name on the line.
e. A: Hi. I'm Joe.
   B: Hi. I'm Barbara.

Page 14
Exercise 3. Listen. Circle the word you hear.
a. A: What's your last name?
   B: My last name is Soto.
b. A: Do you know her name?
   B: Yes. Her name is Mary.
c. A: Write your last name on the form.
   B: Excuse me?
   A: Write your last name.

Page 16
Exercise 3. Listen. Circle the word you hear.
a. A: What's her address?
   B: Her address is 38 Rockwood Road.
   A: Do you know what city that's in?
b. A: He lives on Green Road.
   B: Do you know what number on Green Road?
   A: Number 10.
c. A: What street does Tim live on?
   B: I think he lives on Brown Street.

Page 18
Exercise 3. Listen for *zip code*. Raise your hand.
a. A: What's your zip code?
   B: 33056.
b. A: What's your name?
   B: My name is Tanya.

c. A: My zip code is 87730.
   B: What city is that?
   A: Santa Fe.
d. A: What's your address?
   B: 45 Main Street.

Page 20
Exercise 3. Listen for *telephone number*. Raise your hand.
a. A: What's his address?
   B: 35 Riverside Drive.
b. A: What's your telephone number?
   B: 555-1238.
c. A: What's your last name?
   B: Dalton.
d. A: My telephone number is 503-555-0112.
   B: OK. Thanks.

Page 28
Exercise 3. Listen. Circle the place you hear.
a. A: Where's the police station?
   B: The police station? It's on Green Street.
b. A: I want to mail a letter. Where's the post office?
   B: The post office is on Green Street, I think.
c. A: I think the bank is on Brown Street.
   B: No. The bank's on Green Street.

Page 31
Exercise 5. Listen. Circle the word you hear.
a. A: Excuse me. Could you tell me where the post office is?
   B: Sure. The post office is two blocks down on the right.
   A: Thanks.
b. A: Oh, no. I'm out of stamps.
   B: I have some. How many stamps do you need?
   A: Only two.
   B: Here you go.

A: Thanks.

c. A: We have to mail the letter to George. Where's a mailbox?

B: There's a mailbox on Green Street.

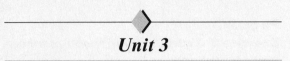

Unit 3

Page 42
Exercise 3. Listen. Circle the word you hear.

a. A: Do you know where the men's room is?

B: Yes. The men's room is on the left, next to room 23.

b. A: Where's the women's room?

B: The women's room is down the hall on the right, next to room 20.

A: Thanks.

c. A: I'm looking for the office.

B: The office is in room 22, on the right.

A: Thanks.

Page 45
Exercise 5. Listen. Circle the number.

a. John, please sit at this desk.

b. Please open your books.

Unit 4

Page 50
Exercise 3. Listen. Circle the times you hear.

a. A: Oh, I'm going to be late for work. What time is it?

B: Don't worry. It's only 7:30.

A: Only 7:30? It's early.

b. A: Excuse me. When does the next train arrive?

B: It should be here at 9:00.

A: 9:00? Thanks.

c. A: There's a movie for the kids at the library tomorrow. Do you want to come?

B: What time?

A: 3:30.

B: That sounds like fun. I'll meet you there at 3:30.

d. A: Wake up! It's 7:00. It's time to get ready for school.

B: I'm tired. Do I have to?

A: Yes. It's 7:00. You have to get up.

Page 53
Exercise 5. Listen. Circle the days you hear.

a. A: Are we in the same English class?

B: I don't know. When's your class?

A: On Tuesday night. How about you?

B: My class is on Tuesday, too. I guess we're in the same class.

b. A: What day do you have off this week?

B: Thursday.

A: Really? Do you want to go to the movies on Thursday?

B: Sure. That'd be great.

c. A: Do you want to go out for lunch on Sunday?

B: I'm sorry, I can't. I usually visit my mother on Sunday.

d. A: My son's playing baseball on Saturday. Can you come to the game?

B: What time does the game start? I work on Saturday morning.

A: 2:00.

B: Great. I'll be there.

Page 54
Exercise 3. Listen. Circle the date you hear.

a. A: Hi, Sally. I want to invite you to a party we're having.

B: Great. When is it?

A: July third.

B: Oh, that's too bad. We'll be away on July third. I'm afraid that we can't come.

A: Sorry you'll have to miss it.

B: Me, too.

b. A: I'm calling to make an appointment with Dr. Martin.

B: When would you like to see her?

A: The second week in June.
B: How's June ninth at 2:00?
A: June ninth is fine. Thanks.
c. A: I sure could use a day off from work.
B: Me, too. We haven't had a day off for a couple of months.
A: Well, Columbus Day is only a few days away.
B: When's that?
A: October twelfth.
B: That's soon enough. October twelfth is next week.
d. A: When can I see the dentist?
B: How about July fifteenth?
A: No. July fifteenth is my birthday. I don't want to go to the dentist on my birthday.

Unit 5

Page 63
Exercise 3. Listen. Circle the number of the food you hear.
a. A: I have to stop at the supermarket.
B: What do you need?
A: A dozen eggs.
b. A: What do you want for dinner tonight?
B: How about chicken? I think I have a chicken in the freezer.
A: That sounds great.
c. A: What's left on the list?
B: A carton of milk.
A: Milk? I'll get it. The dairy section is over there. I'll meet you at the front of the store.

Page 65
Exercise 6. Listen. Circle the aisle number you hear.
a. A: Excuse me. Where's the detergent?
B: Aisle 2.
A: Aisle 2? Thanks.
b. A: We have to get bread and oranges.
B: The fruit and vegetables section is on aisle 3.

A: Where?
B: Aisle 3.
c. A: Let's see. I have to get rice and cereal. Do you know where the cereal is?
B: I'm not sure. Oh look, there's a sign. It says cereal's on aisle 6.
A: Aisle 6. Thanks.

Unit 6

Page 75
Exercise 5. Listen. Circle the number.
a. A: How much are the socks?
B: $2.95.
A: I'll take them.
B: Cash or charge?
A: Cash, please.
b. A: This coat is nice. How much is it?
B: $38.00.
A: Do you take charge cards?
B: Yes, we do.
c. A: The total for your shoes is $21.75. How would you like to pay?
B: Can I write a check?
A: Yes, but I'll need to see some ID.
B: That's fine. I have my license right here.

Page 77
Exercise 5. Listen. Circle the amount you hear.
a. A: How much is the paint?
B: $21.99.
b. A: Will that be cash or check?
B: What was the total?
A: $15.00.
B: I think I'll write a check.
c. A: I'm just going to stop and buy a hammer. They're on sale.
B: Really? How much? I need a hammer, too.
A: $8.50.
B: That's not much of a sale.

Unit 7

Page 86
Exercise 3. Listen. Circle the answer.
a. A: Where do you live, Manuel?
   B: I have an apartment on Green Street.
b. A: I went to Sandra's house yesterday.
   B: Where does she live?
   A: She lives over on Main Street.
   B: What's her house like?
   A: Oh, it's beautiful.
c. A: Hi, Mike. Would you like to go with us to the movies this afternoon?
   B: Yeah. That sounds like fun.
   A: OK. We can pick you up if you like. Where do you live?
   B: 12 Oak Street, apartment 33.
   A: Fine. We'll be there in about an hour.

Page 88
Exercise 3. Listen. Circle the room you hear.
a. A: I'm so tired I can hardly keep my eyes open.
   B: Why don't you go into the bedroom and take a nap?
   A: That's a good idea. I think I will.
b. A: Where's Dad?
   B: I'm not sure. Did you look in the kitchen? Maybe he's cooking dinner.
c. A: We need to clean the house before our party.
   B: I'll clean the bathroom.
   A: OK. I'll vacuum.

Page 90
Exercise 3. Listen. Circle the item you hear.
a. A: May I help you?
   B: Yes. I need a new stove. Do you have any stoves on sale?
   A: Yes. We have several models on sale this week.
b. A: How do you like your new house?

B: It's great. I just need a few pieces of furniture.
   A: What do you need?
   B: Well, to begin with, a new chair for the living room.
c. A: Bell's Appliance Repair. May I help you?
   B: Yes. My refrigerator isn't working. Can someone come by and take a look at it?
   A: Certainly. What's the address?
   B: 12 Oak Street, apartment 33.
   A: We'll send someone over this afternoon.
   B: Thanks.

Page 93
Exercise 5. Listen. Circle *rent* or *deposit*.
a. A: We found a great apartment.
   B: Where?
   A: On Brown Street.
   B: How many bedrooms?
   A: Two bedrooms and one bathroom.
   B: How's the rent?
   A: Pretty good. $425 a month.
b. A: Do you like the apartment?
   B: Yes, but I'm not sure I can afford it. Is there a deposit?
   A: Yes. $175.
   B: $175?
   A: Yes.
c. A: It's not easy to find an apartment for six people.
   B: I know. We were lucky to find one with three bedrooms.
   A: How much is the rent?
   B: $650.
   A: $650? Wow, that's high.

Unit 8

Page 99
Exercise 6. Listen. Circle the word you hear.
a. A: What happened?
   B: He slipped on the wet floor.
   A: Is he OK?

B: No. He hurt his arm. I think we should take him to the emergency room.

b. A: Help!

B: What happened?

A: I cut my hand on the broken glass!

B: Oh, my! That looks pretty bad. We'd better go to the hospital.

c. A: Mom, I cut my foot.

B: Let me see.

A: It hurts.

B: It's not a bad cut. Let me wash it and put a bandage on it.

Page 101
Exercise 6. Listen. When will the people see the doctor? Circle the answers.

a. A: Dr. Franklin's office. May I help you?

B: Yes. I need to make an appointment to have my eyes checked.

A: Can you come in on Tuesday?

B: What time?

A: 10:30.

B: OK. Tuesday at 10:30.

b. A: Can I make an appointment to see the dentist?

B: Sure. How about Wednesday at 10:00?

A: That'll be fine.

B: OK. We'll see you Wednesday, April 16 at 10:00 A.M.

c. A: Do you think you can give me a ride to the clinic?

B: Sure. When do you need to go?

A: I have an appointment Monday at 4:45.

Page 103
Exercise 6. Listen. What's the matter? Circle the answers.

a. A: I think we should take the baby to the doctor.

B: Why?

A: She has a sore throat.

B: Maybe she has a cold.

A: Let's call the doctor and ask.

b. A: I feel awful.

B: What's the matter?

A: I have a terrible headache.

B: Why don't you take some aspirin?

c. A: I have to call the doctor.

B: What's the matter? Are you sick?

A: Yes. I have a really bad stomachache.

Page 104
Exercise 3. Listen. How much medicine do they take? Check the box.

a. A: Jung, you don't look well. Are you sick?

B: Yes. I went to see the doctor this morning.

A: Did she give you any medicine?

B: Yes. She gave me a prescription. I have to take two capsules three times a day.

b. A: I just got a prescription for my cough.

B: How much do you need to take?

A: It says two teaspoons every four hours.

c. A: Here's your prescription, Iris.

B: Thanks. How much do I take?

A: Take two tablets every six hours.

B: OK. Thanks.

d. A: Ms. Parker, here's Pat's prescription.

B: How much does Pat take?

A: Give him two tablespoons every morning before breakfast.

Unit 9

Page 110
Exercise 3. Listen. Circle the job you hear.

a. A: Oh, I'm tired.

B: Why?

A: I have a new job as a cook, and I'm on my feet all day.

B: Well, do you like the work?

A: Yes. Even though it's hard, I enjoy it.

b. A: Have you found a job yet?

B: Yes. I finally got a job at the Shaw Company.

A: Doing what?

B: I'm a file clerk.

A: That sounds great. Congratulations.

c. A: How's your brother?

B: He's fine. He just got a good job.

A: Really? What's he doing?

B: He's an auto mechanic at Silvio's Garage.

Page 112
Exercise 4. Listen. Do they have any work experience? Circle *Yes* or *No.*

a. A: I'm calling about the ad for a gardener.

B: Do you have any experience?

A: Yes. Before I came to this country, I was a gardener for many years.

B: Great. Can you come in later today for an interview?

A: Sure.

b. A: Hope Hospital. May I help you?

B: Yes. I saw your ad for a housekeeper. I'd like to apply for the job. Can you tell me about it?

A: Well, it's a part-time position, and the salary is $5.50 an hour. Do you have any experience?

B: No, I don't. Is that a problem?

A: No, it's OK. Experience isn't required. We have a training program for people without experience.

B: That sounds great.

c. A: Look at this ad, May. It's a perfect job for you.

B: What kind of job is it?

A: The American Cafe is looking for a full-time cook with experience working in a restaurant.

B: That sounds perfect. I worked at the Pickwick Restaurant for three years. Is there a phone number I can call?

Unit 10

Page 122
Exercise 3. Listen. Circle the correct picture.

a. A: Hurry up! The train's coming.

B: We'd better run.

b. A: I have to go downtown tomorrow. Can you give me a ride?

B: I'm sorry, I can't. My car's in the shop getting fixed.

c. A: How are you going to the game?

B: We're going to take the bus.

Page 126
Exercise 2. Listen. Circle the correct sign.

a. A: Be careful when you cross the street.

B: Don't worry. I'll be careful.

A: Only cross when the sign says WALK.

b. A: I saw a terrible accident.

B: What happened?

A: A car went through a stop sign and hit another car.

c. A: You'd better slow down. You're going too fast.

B: No, I'm not. The speed limit's 55.

Page 129
Exercise 5. Listen. Where do the people want to go? Circle the place you hear.

a. A: Excuse me. Does this bus go to the train station?

B: Yes. It leaves for the station every 15 minutes.

A: And could you tell me the fare?

B: That'll be $1.00.

b. A: Which bus do I take to get to City Community College?

B: The blue bus just up ahead will take you there, but you'll have to hurry. It's about to leave.

A: I'd better run then. I hope I have enough money with me. Do you know how much the fare is?

B: $1.25.

A: Thanks.

c. A: Excuse me. Does this bus go to Village Green Mall?

B: Yes. The mall is our first stop.

A: I know the fare is $2.00. Do I need exact change?

B: Yes, you do.

d. A: I got a new job at City Hospital. Do you know what bus I take to get there?

B: The bus on the corner goes to City Hospital.

A: By any chance, do you know how much the fare is?

B: $1.50.

A: Thanks.

Listen again. Write the fare. *[Play the tape or read the transcript for Exercise 5 aloud again.]*

The blackline masters on pages 142–152 allow for additional review and enrichment. Because you can make as many copies as you need, you can use them for a variety of purposes throughout the book:

♦ Students who complete individual, pair, or small group activities before the rest of the class can complete a blackline master activity independently.

♦ In open-entry/open-exit programs, use the blackline masters to provide any needed review as new students join the class.

♦ Use the blackline masters as games or for pair work.

♦ Have students complete a blackline master activity as review before the Check Your Competency page.

♦ You can assign them as homework.

Here are a few specific suggestions on ways you can use each blackline master. Feel free to think of additional activities of your own.

Blackline Master 1: Identification Form

♦ To help students generalize that different forms ask for the same information, have students look at both forms. Say **name** and have them point to it on both forms. Continue with the other information on the forms.

♦ Have students fill out the forms independently.

♦ Have pairs interview each other and complete one of the forms for their partners.

Blackline Master 2: Telephone

♦ Have students practice dialing telephone numbers. Say telephone numbers aloud and have students touch the numbers on the keypad. Use the numbers of businesses, service agencies, long distance numbers, 800 numbers, 911, directory assistance, the school's office or attendance office, their employers (for reporting absences), the poison control center, and so on. Individuals might say their telephone numbers for the others to dial.

♦ To reinforce letters of the alphabet, have students look at the telephone and find which letters are not on the keypad (**Q** and **Z**).

♦ To reinforce letters and/or numbers, use correction fluid to delete several letters and/or numbers on a photocopy of the master. Then duplicate a copy for every student. Have students fill in the missing information.

Blackline Master 3: Classroom Objects

♦ Have students cut out the pictures and use them to start personal picture dictionaries or to make flash cards. (For instructions, see page vii of the Introduction to the Literacy Level.)

♦ Have students label the pictures.

♦ Divide the class into teams. Give each team a copy of the blackline master. Have each team collect as many of the actual objects as they can. Have each team report how many of each object they have, "We have (three) erasers."

Blackline Master 4: Clock

♦ Give each student a copy of the blackline master. Help them cut out the hands and mount them with brads. Then say times and have students display the time on their clocks. Check to make sure everyone has the correct time.

Blackline Master 5: Money

♦ Use the money to teach students how to say amounts of money. Display various amounts and say how much money you have, such as three hundred dollars. Have students repeat.

♦ Set up a classroom store, supermarket, or mall. Students can use the money to pay for purchases.

Blackline Master 6: Blank Check

♦ Use an overhead transparency of the master to model how to write and endorse checks.

♦ Make multiple copies and have students use them to "pay" various bills, such as utility bills, rent payments, and so on. You might bring in, or have students bring in, real bills for them to look at and pay with the checks.

♦ Bring in mail order catalogs. Have the class imagine that they are going to buy an item. Help them make a selection, complete the order form, and pay with one of the checks.

Blackline Masters 7a and b: House and Furniture

♦ Give each student copies of the masters. Give instructions about how to place the furniture in the rooms. When everyone has finished, have pairs compare their arrangements to make sure that they are the same.

♦ Have students use the furniture pictures in their personal picture dictionaries. (See page vii of the Introduction to the Literacy Level.)

♦ Have students use the money from **Blackline Master 5** and the furniture and to set up a furniture store. Help students put prices on the furniture. Give each student a certain amount of money, such as $500, to furnish their homes. Have them go shopping in pairs or in small groups, make their purchases, and pay for them. Appoint clerks to help the customers. Have students arrange their purchases in their homes and describe them to the class.

Blackline Master 8: Human Body

♦ Have students use a copy of the blackline master in their personal picture dictionaries. (See page vii of the Introduction to the Literacy Level.)

♦ Use the blackline master to play a variety of Simon Says games. For example, give each student a copy of the unlabeled human body.

Say, "Simon says, 'Point to the head.'" Have students respond by pointing to the head. Any students who follow an instruction not prefaced by "Simon says" must stop playing.

You might also have students play using the labeled human body. Give instructions as before and have students point to the correct word except when the instruction is not prefaced by "Simon says."

♦ To reinforce listening and writing skills, give each student a copy of the unlabeled picture. Dictate the names of the body parts in random order and have students write them on the correct lines. Check students' work.

Blackline Master 9: Job Application

♦ Have students complete the application about themselves. Then collect the completed applications, check them, and return them to students with another copy of the application. Have them complete the second application with the corrected information. Check their work. Remind them to carry this application with them when applying for jobs to help them complete the applications quickly and accurately.

♦ Have pairs interview each other and complete the application for their partners.

Blackline Master 10: Bus Schedule

♦ Have students look over the map and schedule. Have them use it to plan trips to various places and at various times of day. Check to make sure that all of the trips are possible.

♦ Students might use the map and schedule as a model to create maps and schedules for a real or imaginary bus route in their city or town.

Each unit of the Teacher's Edition contains additional ideas for using the blackline masters.

IDENTIFICATION FORM

Name	
Address	
City	State
Zip Code	Telephone Number

IDENTIFICATION FORM

NAME

ADDRESS

CITY   STATE   ZIP CODE

TELEPHONE NUMBER

142

IMPORTANT TELEPHONE NUMBERS	
Police	**911**
Fire Department	**911**
Ambulance	**911**

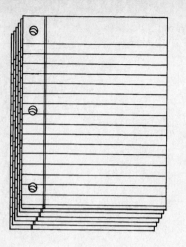

Blackline Master 3: Classroom Objects

Blackline Master 4: Clock

550

_____ 19 _____

PAY TO THE
ORDER OF _____ $ [   ]

_____ DOLLARS

✳**CITY**BANK
CITYBANK of AMERICA

MEMO

551

_____ 19 _____

PAY TO THE
ORDER OF _____ $ [   ]

_____ DOLLARS

✳**CITY**BANK
CITYBANK of AMERICA

MEMO

ENDORSE HERE

X

DO NOT WRITE BELOW THIS LINE

Blackline Master 6: Blank Check

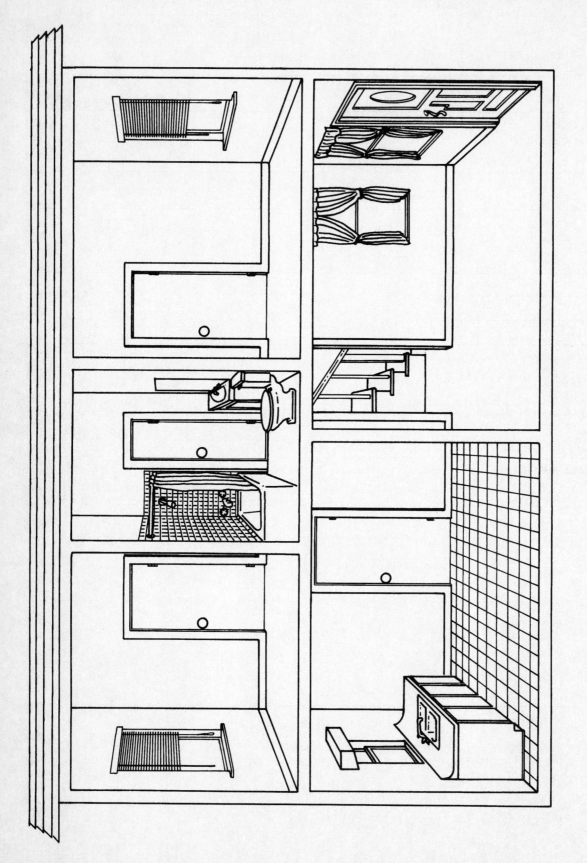

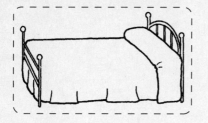

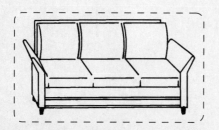
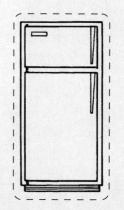

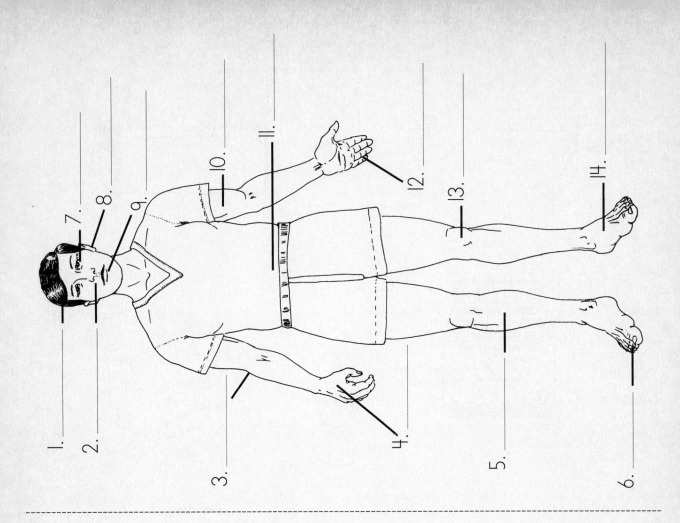

1.
2.
3.
4.
5.
6.
7.
8.
9.
10.
11.
12.
13.
14.

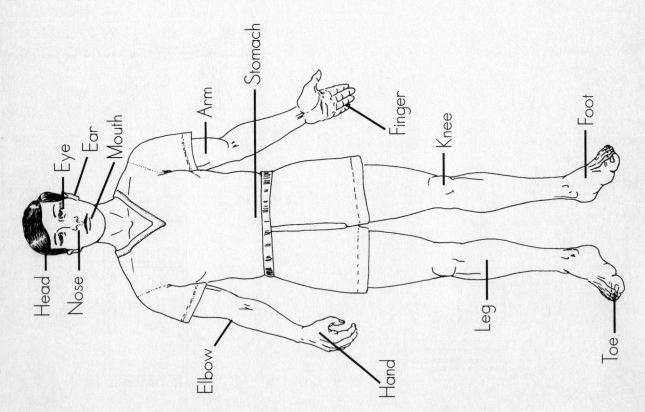

Head
Eye
Nose
Ear
Mouth
Arm
Stomach
Elbow
Hand
Finger
Knee
Leg
Foot
Toe

THE Star COMPANY

APPLICATION FOR EMPLOYMENT

Name:	
Social Security Number:	Telephone Number:
Address:	
Position applied for:	Date you can start:

Salary expected:

_____ an hour _____ a month _____ a year

☐ Full time

☐ Part time—If part time, hours you can work:

Monday—Friday: _____ Saturday/Sunday: _____

List any friends and/or relatives working with us now:

Are you over 21? Yes ☐ No ☐

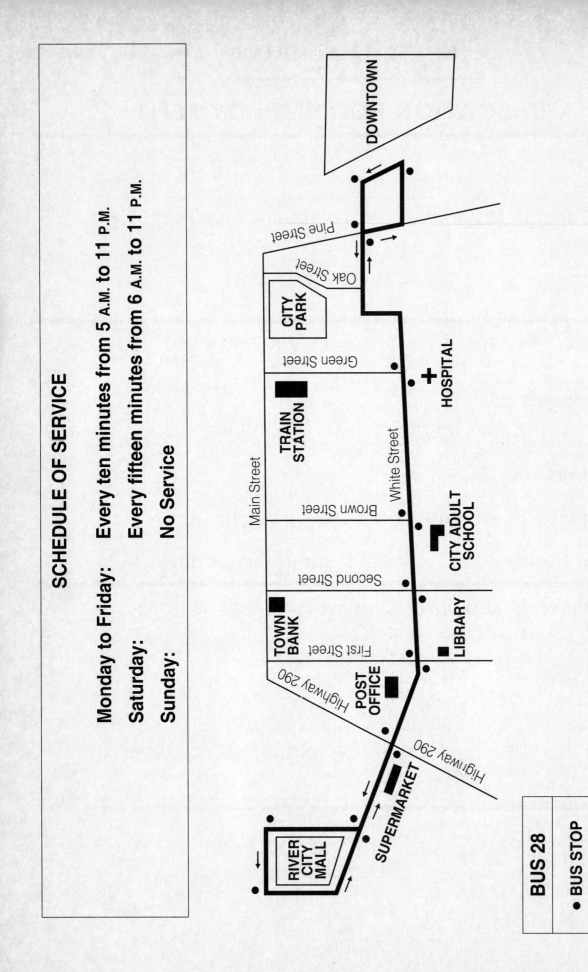

SCHEDULE OF SERVICE

Monday to Friday: **Every ten minutes from 5 A.M. to 11 P.M.**

Saturday: **Every fifteen minutes from 6 A.M. to 11 P.M.**

Sunday: **No Service**

DOWNTOWN

Pine Street

Oak Street

CITY PARK

Green Street

HOSPITAL

TRAIN STATION

White Street

Main Street

Brown Street

CITY ADULT SCHOOL

Second Street

LIBRARY

TOWN BANK

First Street

Highway 290

POST OFFICE

Highway 290

SUPERMARKET

RIVER CITY MALL

BUS 28

● **BUS STOP**

Blackline Master 10: Bus Map and Schedule

Art Glass Quilts

New Subtractive Appliqué Technique

JULIE HIROTA

Text and Artwork © 2004 Julie Hirota
Artwork © 2004 C&T Publishing

Publisher: Amy Marson
Editorial Director: Gailen Runge
Editor: Lynn Koolish
Technical Editors: Terry Stroin, Joyce Lytle, Carolyn Aune
Copyeditor/Proofreader: Eva Simoni Erb/Stacy Chamness
Cover Designer: Christina D. Jarumay
Design Director/Book Designer: Christina D. Jarumay
Illustrator: Matt Allen
Production Assistant: Timothy Manibusan
Quilt Photography: Steven Buckley, Photographic Reflections unless
otherwise noted
How-to Photography: Luke Mulks
Published by C&T Publishing, Inc., P.O. Box 1456, Lafayette, California,
94549

Front cover: *Flower Arranging*
Back cover: *Martini Lunch, Go Fishing, and Laurel Crown*

Library of Congress Cataloging-in-Publication Data
Hirota, Julie.
   Art glass quilts : new subtractive appliqué technique / Julie Hirota.
      p. cm.
   ISBN 1-57120-260-9
   1. Quilting. 2. Patchwork. I. Title.
   TT835.H5336 2004
   746.46–dc22
                              2004001395

Printed in China
10 9 8 7 6 5 4 3 2 1

TABLE

OF
CONTENTS

ACKNOWLEDGMENTS

The constant encouragement and cheerleading of my family and close friends made this book possible. Each and every one of you deserves my sincerest thanks. Thank you to the Foothill Quilters Guild for introducing me to many experts in color theory, quilting workmanship, and design. I appreciate the opportunity to learn from you. A special thank you to the Northern California regional Studio Art Quilt Associates. You inspired me to build my portfolio and my profession. Thank you to the staff at C&T, your hard work and professionalism made this experience so pleasing. Finally, thank you Marne. You recognized something in me that took too much time for me to recognize myself.

DEDICATION

For Gracie, you gave me the opportunity to explore a new world. I would have never taken the leap without you.

For Aaron, you give me eternal support, encouragement, and confidence in my new world.

INTRODUCTION

The creative impulses that hid beneath the surface throughout my early life manifested themselves in college. I experimented with various forms of tactile art, including traditional quiltmaking. Following college, I still longed for creativity in my life. After a full day of work in the high-tech world, I spent my evenings and spare time experimenting with numerous forms of fiber art. I made many quilts, and saw my quiltmaking evolve. I started by making traditional quilts, and later aimed for a contemporary style with freedom and lots of color. Wanting to focus my full-time attention on something I loved—I devoted my newfound life to quiltmaking. I developed Subtractive Appliqué™, a loosely structured appliqué method that incorporates contemporary styles, freedom, and color.

Getting Started

WHAT IS SUBTRACTIVE APPLIQUÉ?

I'm often told that my quilts look like art glass or stained glass. This came quite unexpectedly. In fact, both pop art influences and my drawing instructor led me to experiment with line drawings. I began to create small-scale drawings, with my favorite drawing tool from class: a felt-tip pen. When I enlarged the drawings on the computer, I discovered an unexpected result. The magnified lines from the felt-tip pen became bold and thick. Although I had planned to use the lines as guidelines to separate objects, I liked their boldness, so I incorporated the lines as style elements instead. These thick lines became my trademark.

After I decided to incorporate the lines into my quilts, the next step was to fill the open spaces, or "windows" with color. This came quite easily. The windows provided an opportunity to showcase a variety of fabrics. This was quite exciting and became the inspiration for my technique, Subtractive Appliqué. With this versatile approach, quilt-makers at any level can achieve remarkable results.

The chapters of this book show easy steps for constructing an original quilt, and include patterns that let you practice the Subtractive Appliqué techniques. You will learn to:

■ Understand the principles needed to design a visually balanced quilt

■ Create and apply a precise framework to do beautifully turned edges for Subtractive Appliqué

■ Add borders, quilt, and finish the piece for a visually stunning quilt

Get ready to be excited by this fun approach to appliqué. The technique will make your quilts look like you've been appliquéing all your life!

The Right Tool for the Job

Time spent finding the best tool for a job is time well spent. You probably already know that quiltmaking is more enjoyable when you have tools you like and use regularly. I have experimented with numerous tools and materials to find the ones that work well for me for Subtractive Appliqué. Experiment with these preferred tools and materials, and decide which you like best.

Tools and supplies

Tools

Miniature iron Use this small iron to press the seam allowances. It's lightweight and easier to handle for long periods.

Small embroidery scissors Good, sharp scissors are essential to cut shapes and trim appliqué; small ones allow you to be precise.

Craft knife A large X-ACTO or similar craft knife is the best tool I've found to cut the layers of interfacing and freezer paper.

Stiletto The sharp point of a stiletto helps you press and turn seam allowances.

Even-feed walking foot Use this foot for quilting, or use the built-in even-feed foot if your sewing machine has one.

Rotary cutter, ruler, and mat These tools help deliver precision and speed when you cut pieced borders, bindings, batting, and backings.

Paper and pencil A must for every quilt designer. You will use them for designing and writing notes.

Felt-tip pen A medium point is best to use for tracing designs.

Glue stick Use a glue stick to temporarily attach the window fabrics (inserted appliqué shapes) to the outline fabrics. If you prefer, use glass-head pins as a substitute.

Glass-head pins Use pins to attach the window fabrics (inserted appliqué shapes) to the outline fabrics, as an alternative to a glue stick. Glass-head pins are tough and can be ironed.

Freezer paper Use freezer paper to stabilize the fusible interfacing. Purchase the widest (usually 18") and longest roll of freezer paper available.

Medium-weight fusible interfacing Pellon ShirtTailor works the best for Subtractive Appliqué. This non-woven interfacing won't permanently bond to freezer paper, but stabilizes the fabric well.

Starch Use spray starch to loosen the fabric fibers before you press, and to hold pressed seams in place.

Thread Use monofilament thread for the top stitching, standard sewing thread for the bobbin, and a heavy-weight thread for quilting.

Butcher paper or pattern drafting paper Draw the enlarged design on either type of paper. Professional pattern drafting paper is available through the garment-making industry at specialty stores or by mail order (see Resources on page 79). It has preprinted 1" measurements and is a good substitute for Tru-Grid (see Enlarging Aids, below).

Enlarging Aids

Before you purchase any of the tools to enlarge a design, refer to the enlarging options on pages 23–24 to determine what method you prefer.

Tru-Grid Use this soft pattern material made by Pellon to enlarge the designs using the grid enlargement method. It has a 1" grid printed on it that makes it perfect for enlarging and is available at many fabric stores.

Graph paper Use $1/4$" graph paper to draw a small-scale design. The graph paper will make it easy to enlarge the design using Tru-Grid.

Overhead projector An overhead projector, if available, is a useful tool for enlarging drawings.

Transparency film Transparency film is used with the overhead projector.

FABRIC SELECTION

Outline and *window* fabrics refer to specific parts of Subtractive Appliqué quilts. The outline fabric appears as the lines, and the window fabrics are the contrasting colored fabrics inserted between the lines. Although I generally use solid black cotton as my outline fabric, I have used other colors and prints that read as a solid fabric. Outline fabrics of different colors produce quite distinctive results. You can vary the outline fabrics to create combinations you prefer. (See page 17 for a color practice exercise on how the outline color affects the overall look of the quilt.)

Outline and window fabrics

Window

Outline

Collect a Stash

I often make trips to the fabric stores because a fabulous fabric always inspires me. I usually purchase only one or two special fabrics, but when I see all the new seasonal colors and fabric lines, I find new favorites and reevaluate my growing stash with new eyes. In order to collect more fabrics that work with my palette, I bring an index card with swatches of the colors that I have in my collection. My index card keeps me focused and makes it easy to search for the things I need among all those new temptations.

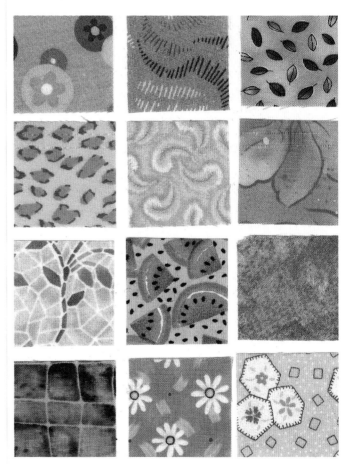

Bring an index card with swatches of fabric colors you already have, so you know what values and hues are missing from your stash.

Like any collector, I am drawn to the fabrics I like best. I collect bold colors, polka dots, and batiks, but these fabrics alone do not make a quilt visually appealing enough that it will "dance" before your eyes; you need a more varied collection of fabrics. To build a collection with a wide variety of printed fabrics, you need to analyze what you have and do not have in terms of color, value, and pattern. You need to include both large- and small-scale patterns; to add pizzazz, collect bold geometrics, stripes, and polka dots. There are always new batiks, novelty and ethnic prints, and vibrant hand-dyed fabrics in a multitude of hues and values.

Bright prints and patterns

Don't forget to include subtle neutrals, pastels, and muted hues in the collection as well. (See pages 16–17 for more on color.)

Subtle neutrals, pastels, and muted hues

You may want to set aside traditional calico or home-spun fabrics for other projects. Their patterns are compact, repetitious, and less interesting. If you use a bright palette as I do, calicoes often appear gray next to vibrant fabrics.

I don't buy all new fabrics for a newly designed quilt and I don't always have "just the right fabric" in my stash. Sometimes, I will dye, print, or embellish a fabric to create a more intriguing piece of material; other times I try a completely different fabric than I had originally intended. It's surprising how often I like the different fabric and the new direction it takes the quilt. In my original sketches and designs, I envisioned *Reuben* to have a green polka-dotted background. However, I didn't have any green polka-dotted fabric I liked. Instead, I used some of my favorite gray-blue-lavender polka dots. This took the background to a light blue instead of green. Fortunately, this worked very well, and overall, the quilt was a success.

In *Reuben* an alternative fabric choice worked beautifully.

FABRIC PREPARATION

There are various opinions about prewashing fabrics. Manufacturers strive to minimize or prevent dyes from bleeding in commercial fabrics, so in general, I don't prewash my fabric. I like to work with crisp fabric, and often, I want to use it as soon as I get it home. Be aware, you may still need to wash and even pretreat some fabrics that are more likely to bleed. For instance, hand-dyed, marbled, and batik fabrics are unpredictable. Check all fabrics for bleeding by putting a small swatch of fabric in a glass of lukewarm water. If you see any color in the water, the fabric is bleeding and should be pretreated with an anti-bleeding rinse such as Retayne (available at many quilt shops).

THREADS, NEEDLES, AND TENSION

There is a fine balance between the thread, tension, and needle for ideal stitches. Experiment with the threads that appeal to you, and see how they behave in your sewing machine. Adjust the tension settings to produce beautiful stitches with each different thread. Always match the sewing machine needle type and size to the threads and fabrics you use in the projects. Remember this simple rule: when you sew with a heavier thread, you will need a larger needle. If you use rayon or metallic threads, you'll need embroidery or metallic needles. Following these guidelines can prevent much frustration.

Discard old needles after each project. The sewing machine will operate better, and you will be rewarded with clean, beautiful stitches.

The following chart provides thread, needle, and tension recommendations. Remember, each sewing machine's sensitivity varies, and these are just starting points. To get the best results, get acquainted with how your sewing machine responds to different threads, tensions, and needles.

THREAD, NEEDLE, AND TENSION RECOMMENDATIONS

THREAD	NEEDLE	TENSION
Monofilament for appliqué	80/12 Universal	Lower (3-4)
Buttonhole thread for quilting	100/16 Universal or 90/14 Denim	Higher (6-7)

SEWING MACHINE MAINTENANCE

A well-oiled and maintained machine prevents many problems. Clean and oil the sewing machine after every four hours of sewing. Carefully inspect all the surfaces and look under the throat plate for lint buildup. To prevent lint buildup, routinely clean all the areas and surfaces indicated by the sewing machine manufacturer's instructions. A well cared for machine will perform quietly with strong, even stitches.

SET UP A WORKSPACE

Many of us have to find a way to fit our sewing spaces into our homes. I spent several years sewing on my kitchen table in my one bedroom apartment. A few years ago, I converted my formal dining room into my home studio. I had spent no time in the dining room entertaining, and most of my time there sewing!

If possible, find a space and make it *your* space. This is your creative area—fill it with ideas and things that inspire you. Take the time to get your sewing machine set up so that it is comfortable and appropriate for your height and size.

My home studio

Photo by Bob Perrin

A useful element to consider adding to your creative space is a design wall. I love mine. You won't believe how much this small investment can impact a quilt's design. If you view a quilt on a wall, (as opposed to on the floor or table) you will get much more information about its composition, balance, and impact. Make a place for a simple 5' x 5' design wall. My design wall is made from Styrofoam insulation material covered with batting.

My design wall is permanently attached to the wall, but it is also possible to construct a smaller, portable design board that can be stored when not in use. To do this, use a large sheet of foam-core board (available at art supply stores) covered with batting.

Design wall

Photo by Bob Perrin

Design Basics

It's important to understand design principles, whether you are designing your own quilt or selecting fabrics for one of the projects from this book.

Learn to trust your own design instincts. Practice this by noticing everyday arrangements that are pleasing to your eye. Then analyze them with respect to balance and the six elements of design.

WHAT IS GOOD DESIGN?

Believe it or not, we all know the answer to this! Good design is very personal and intuitive. As you observe and appreciate the placement of lines on a page, objects on a table, or images in a painting, you'll realize what good design means to you. To some, good design is symmetrical and simple, while to others it is busy and complex. Although my design style varies, I approach my work with the following common design fundamentals.

BALANCE

Balance is one of the most important aspects of a quilt design. You can achieve balance in a variety of ways. Mainly, you control the visual balance of a piece through object and value placement. I apply two types of balance in my work:

▦ Symmetrical balance: an identical pattern, or mirror image, repeated on both sides of a middle line.

▦ Asymmetrical balance: an irregular distribution of objects that achieve overall visual balance through their placement.

For example, *Four Patch Evolution* uses a mirror-image symmetrical design. *Into My Garden,* on the other hand, counterbalances several small objects with a few large objects to achieve asymmetrical balance.

Four Patch Evolution uses symmetrical balance. (See quilt on page 60.)

Into My Garden uses asymmetrical balance. (See quilt on page 56.)

You also can use the "rule of thirds" to achieve good balance. The rule of thirds states: divide the frame into thirds both horizontally and vertically, and place the object(s) where those lines intersect. Of course, all rules were meant to be broken; you may only want to use this one until you become confident with balance.

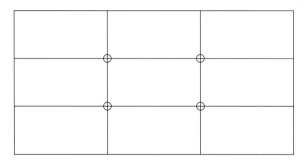

To balance a design using the rule of thirds, place objects where the lines intersect.

In *Butterflies* good balance is achieved by placing the predominant objects on intersection points.

THE SIX ELEMENTS OF DESIGN

Each element of design contributes to and/or affects the balance of a piece. The six elements of design are: line, shape, value, color, pattern, and texture. When these elements combine effectively in a quilt, your eyes will move across the piece and not settle on one part, one color, or one fabric. Use the six elements successfully and you will design a visually stimulating quilt.

Line

Lines define or outline objects. For Subtractive Appliqué, the line drawing forms the central object or image, or it creates a shape. When I sketch my quilts, I create a line drawing with my felt-tip pen. Often, I add additional lines to break up the large spaces and add interest to the design, even if the lines don't define any object.

In *Mothers Day III* additional lines break up the large background spaces and add movement to the quilt. (See quilt on page 57.)

Shape

Connected lines create shapes. A group of disconnected lines in series can also create shapes. It's important to view the design from a distance to determine if there is an imbalance in the piece. If the shapes created by the disconnected lines are too large or small compared to the rest of the images, the design may seem unbalanced. I try to make my background shapes similar to each other in size. This keeps the emphasis on the central image.

In *Field of Flowers* the background shapes are similar to each other in size. (See quilt on page 46.)

Value

Value is the lightness or darkness of color. Using fabrics of all the same value can flatten a stunning design. Similarly, you can create an imbalance if you use extreme value changes in the same object (for example, the background). In general, if you use strong value contrast between the central image and the background, the quilt will be vibrant.

Lazy Daisy shows strong value contrast between the central image and the background.

> *To increase the value contrast of any quilt, you can add a pieced border. (See page 32–34 for Pieced Borders.)*

Color

There are many wonderful books written for quilters about color. Although I've read the rules and studied many color and design lessons, I've found that color theory can be boiled down to a few simple approaches. As a starting point, consider your personal color preferences. Select your favorite color combinations to create a working palette. Refer to your inspirational journal pages that contain an assortment of fabric swatches, pictures, and magazine clippings. (See pages 19–20 for Collecting and Journaling.)

Another method for color selection is to use color schemes such as:

▨ Complementary—colors that are opposite each other on the color wheel

▨ Triadic—any three colors that are equidistant on the color wheel

▨ Tetradic—any four colors that are equidistant on the color wheel

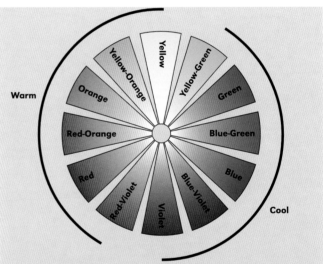

The color wheel is divided into warm and cool colors.

COMPLEMENTARY COLOR COMBINATIONS:
- Yellow and Violet
- Green and Red
- Blue and Orange
- Yellow-Green and Red-Violet
- Blue-Green and Red-Orange
- Blue-Violet and Yellow-Orange

TRIADIC COLOR COMBINATIONS:
- Yellow, Blue, and Red
- Green, Violet, and Orange
- Yellow-Green, Blue-Violet, and Red-Orange
- Blue-Green, Red-Violet, and Yellow-Orange

TETRADIC COLOR COMBINATIONS:
- Yellow, Blue-Green, Violet, and Red-Orange
- Yellow-Green, Blue, Red-Violet, and Orange
- Green, Blue-Violet, Red, and Yellow-Orange

Warm and cool hues provide another starting point in color selection. Warm colors tend to come forward while cool colors recede. Notice how warm-colored objects are amplified and pop forward from a cool-colored background in *Lazy Daisy*.

It's also okay to make color decisions intuitively throughout the process, changing your mind numerous times. The more experience you have with color selection, the more confident and familiar you will be with your own likes and dislikes. I use a lot of black outline fabric in my quilts, but sometimes a palette I like doesn't work well next to the black. When this happens, I change colors and vary the values until I establish a successful color combination.

Expand your palette and use a range of hues within the quilt and a variety of values for each object. For instance, in *Into My Garden* (below), I used several yellow printed fabrics for the sunflower petals, and ten to fifteen green fabrics for the leaves. The variety of hues, fabrics, and values adds interest, and creates a sense of movement in the composition; it "dances".

To create interest, use a variety of values and prints from a color family.

Practice

Color Practice

Use this exercise to create a color and pattern palette for a design. It will help you understand how fabric color, value, and scale work in design.

MATERIALS

1 piece of 3" x 6" white fabric for background
1 piece of 3" x 6" black fabric for background
3 colors of fabrics (for example, green, purple, orange). Select a dark value, a light value, and a bold print of each color, for a total of 9 fabrics.

EXERCISE

1. From each colored fabric cut 2 swatches $1^1/2$" x $1^1/2$" for a total of 18 swatches.
2. Place 3 different colors on the white background and 3 on the black background.
3. Look at each combination, compare the white fabric outline with the black fabric outline.
4. Continue to change and swap values and prints on the two backgrounds until you find combinations you like.

■ Notice how the black outline gives the fabrics a much richer look, and the white outline gives the fabrics a cleaner look.
■ Notice how different prints disappear or emerge based on their scale.

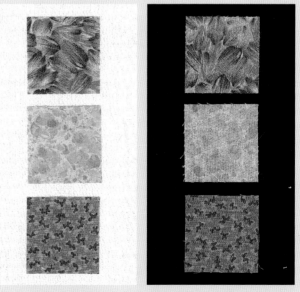

Compare how each fabric looks next to white and black.

Pattern

All fabrics, except solids, have a pattern. Many prints have regular or repeated patterns, while other fabrics have mottled or random designs. In a quilt, patterned fabrics break up the large spaces and define the small spaces. Patterns such as large prints, batiks, hand dyes, and polka dots all have their place. Search for and collect bold prints, busy fabrics, stripes, and polka dots to develop your pattern palette for each quilt. Use a variety of patterns in each color to suggest movement in the quilt. Be careful not to overuse your favorites. Although I love polka dots and batiks, I don't place them everywhere in the same quilt.

> *Don't overuse any one pattern in a quilt; it tends to either flatten or busy the piece.*

Often, the pattern on the fabric isn't suitable for a certain space. For instance, a hand-dyed piece or small print may look drab in a large area. To get a winning combination, I'll stamp or paint the piece to make it more interesting. Almost every quilt I make contains fabrics that I have stamped, painted, printed, or foiled.

You'll find that pattern can greatly change the mood of a quilt. It's difficult to determine ahead of time how you'll use each patterned fabric in a quilt. Collect fabrics with a range of patterns in various colors and you will have many options.

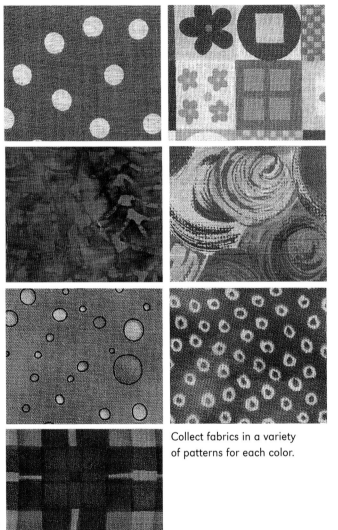

Collect fabrics in a variety of patterns for each color.

Red uses monoprinted lines and foiled dots on a hand-dyed fabric to make this piece more interesting.

The impact of large, bold design is lost when a fabric is cut too small. Likewise, tiny prints completely disappear if they are used in a large area. As a general rule, if the pattern is small, use it in small spaces; if the pattern is large, use it in large open spaces.

Large bold prints lose their impact in small spaces.

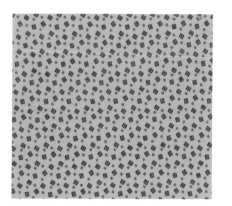

Tiny prints disappear in large spaces.

Texture

Quilting creates texture in a quilt. Texture refers to the appearance and feel of a quilt's surface. Texture is what sets quilts apart from most two-dimensional art. Texture in a quilt changes the piece visually. It can guide you to look from left to right or top to bottom. The feeling of movement in a quilt can be enhanced by the addition of quilting. Notice how the texture of the quilted lines in *Fishes* gives a sense of the fish moving through the water.

The quilting stitches in *Fishes* create a sense of movement.

COLLECTING AND JOURNALING

Before you begin the design process, you'll need some inspiration. That first inspirational moment is often what moves us to create a quilt or try out a new color scheme. Inspiration can come from many directions and quite unexpectedly. To trigger ideas, examine nature and photographs, watch people, and look at drawings, illustrations, fabric swatches, and advertisements. Collect and document your inspirations in a journal to capture them for future use. Jot down why you chose each. Don't worry about how it looks or the order of the entries—just get the ideas documented. Also, observe and collect things you don't like, such as certain color combinations or styles. Write in your journal your reasons for the dislikes.

Practice

Design Practice

Use this exercise to practice creating balance in a design.

MATERIALS

Cutouts of objects from magazines or illustrations that
range in size from ¹/₂" to 2"
Several sheets of 8¹/₂" x 11" white paper
Glue stick

EXERCISE

1. Arrange 3-5 cutouts
of various sizes
horizontally across
the paper.

Cutouts arranged
horizontally

2. On another sheet of
paper, arrange 3-5 cutouts
of various sizes vertically.

Cutouts arranged
vertically

3. Pin up your arrangements on the wall, and view
each composition separately. Ask yourself these
questions:

▪ Does the visual weight of the composition lead my
eye to one place?
▪ Does the composition appear uneven or unbalanced because of the sizes and placement of the
cutouts?

4. If you answer, "yes" to either question, continue to
modify the arrangement and the shapes of the
cutouts until you are satisfied with each composition.

Structure the journal any way you like. Try creating
various style pages. For instance, on one page you
may want to include photos and clippings of a certain
palette. On another page, you can collect images from
a certain period.

I revisit my journal when I'm indecisive about a current
or new project. I typically collect simple patterns and
striking designs. My collection of old sketches, objects,
or photos from magazines preserves those inspirations.
It's interesting to review ideas from years past to see
how they have changed along with the work. I'm
amazed at how quickly my style and color preferences
change. I'm also surprised by how much the current
trends influence my taste.

I also use my journal to keep track of quilt designs and fabric selections.

COMPOSE A DESIGN

You don't have to know how to draw to design. Many
times, when I can't decide how to design a quilt, I
arrange illustrations from my journal on a page to create the design. Use your journal and the information on
balance (pages 13-14) to compose a simple design.

*Don't get stuck thinking you must know how to
draw to design a quilt. Existing illustrations such
as magazine pictures or graphic art can provide
a good starting point.*

MAKE A DRAWING

After you've designed a visually pleasing and balanced composition, you can use it to create your own quilt design. You will need to simplify and reduce the details in the objects because the lines become $1/2"$–$5/8"$ wide when they are enlarged for the full-size quilt. Reducing the amount of detail also gives your fabric selections more impact and makes objects easier to see.

Original fish design

Fish with less detail

Although it's impossible to predict how much detail to remove until the piece is enlarged, it's easier to eliminate detail in the small drawing than in the enlarged one. Look at the quilts in the gallery (pages 43-60) to get a sense of what type of detail to keep and what to remove.

Once you have removed detail and finished the drawing, you may need to add additional interest to the composition. Extend natural lines that occur in the objects, or add lines to break up the area in the background. The lines can end suddenly or extend to the edge of the drawing. Additional fabrics will fill the new spaces you create with the added lines.

You can now use your drawing to create your own quilt! Read on to learn how.

Natural lines and additional lines break up the space and add interest.

Prepare
the Framework

The following steps show how to transfer and enlarge a design—either from this book or from your own drawing. You will enlarge the design, trace it onto freezer paper, cut out the pattern, and transfer it to the outline fabric. Be sure to read all the instructions and do the practice exercises before starting a quilt.

*The **outline** appears as the solid lines. The **window** fabrics are the contrasting colored fabrics inserted between the lines.*

Trace the Design

The selected design needs to be a mirror image of the original design before you enlarge it. Then when you apply the enlarged image to the wrong side of the outline fabric, the final piece will be in the original orientation.

Preparation for Enlarging

If you are using your own design, you need to trace the mirror image of the design before enlarging. Use a light table or a window to trace the design on a piece of paper. I trace right onto the back of the same piece of paper that has the completed design on it. A felt-tip pen with a medium tip will give you the best line width when enlarged. If you are working on a project from the book, the mirror image is provided; no reversing is necessary.

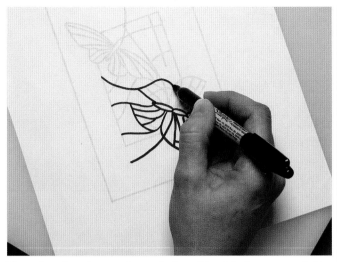

Trace the mirror image of your design with a felt-tip pen on a light table before enlarging.

*It's easiest to mirror (trace the reverse of) a design **before** you enlarge it.*

ENLARGE THE DESIGN

After you trace the design, the next step is to enlarge it. There are several ways to do this. The first process is the one I almost always use, followed by several alternatives. Use what's easiest for you. The projects at the end of the book indicate how much to enlarge each design.

Enlarge With a Scanner

I like to use my desktop scanner to enlarge my designs. For me, it's the quickest and easiest.

1. Decide the finished size of the quilt.

2. Determine the percentage to enlarge the design. For example, if the design is 8" x 10" and the finished quilt is 24" x 30", enlarge the design 300%. To determine how much to enlarge the design, use this simple formula:

(finished width [or height] of quilt ÷ drawing width [or height]) x 100 = % to enlarge.

The scanning software makes enlarging easy—it asks for the percentage to enlarge.

3. Scan the design.

4. Print out the design on 8$\frac{1}{2}$" x 11" paper. You will need to print the design in sections because it's larger than the paper. Refer to the instructions for your drawing or scanning program to determine how to print out a large image in sections. Carefully tape the sections together to form the pattern.

Carefully tape the printed sections together.

Enlarge at a Copy Shop

The most conventional way to enlarge a drawing is through a blueprint or copy shop. Some shops can enlarge the drawing to your desired size on a single sheet of paper. Otherwise, enlarge the drawing in sections as needed.

Enlarge with a Grid

The most accessible way to enlarge a drawing is to use a grid.

1. Trace the reversed design onto $\frac{1}{4}$" graph paper. Each square on the graph paper will represent 1" on the Tru-Grid (or other product with 1" grid lines). Be sure to draw the design with the enlarged ratio in mind. That is, each $\frac{1}{4}$" square on the graph paper represents 1" on the Tru-Grid so your design will be enlarged 4 times or 400%. For example, a 5" x 7" drawing enlarges to 20" x 28" using this method.

2. Copy each square from the graph paper onto Tru-Grid or another 1" gridded sheet. (See page 7 for more on Tru-Grid.)

3. When complete, use a $1/2$" flexible curve to make the drawn lines smooth and a consistent width.

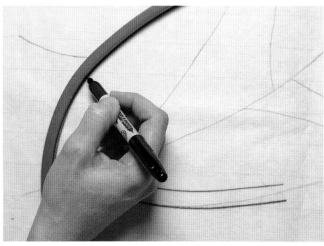

A $1/2$" flexible curve will help with enlarging your design.

Enlarge with an Overhead Projector

Overhead projectors are often available through schools and local libraries.

1. Trace the reversed design onto transparency acetate rather than paper.

2. Project the transparency onto paper that is taped to a wall. Move the projector closer or further away until the design is the desired size. Distortion, also called keystoning, can occur if the projector face is not perfectly parallel to the tracing wall. To minimize this, draw a box around the design on the transparency acetate. Adjust the projector until the top and the bottom of the box are the same length and the sides are the same length.

3. Trace the projected image onto the paper.

4. When complete, use a $1/2$" flexible curve to make the drawn lines smooth and a consistent width.

PREPARE THE FREEZER PAPER

Now, use the enlarged design as a pattern to trace onto freezer paper.

1. Place a piece of freezer paper *dull* side up on top of the enlarged pattern. Make sure that the freezer paper covers the entire pattern. If the freezer paper is too small, create a larger piece by attaching pieces of freezer paper together using transparent tape on the dull side.

2. Trace the pattern onto the dull side of the freezer paper.

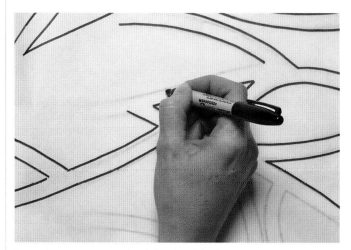

Trace the pattern onto the dull side of the freezer paper.

CREATE LACE

In Subtractive Appliqué, "lace" is the term I use for freezer paper and fusible interfacing layered together. The freezer paper stabilizes the interfacing so it cuts easily with a craft knife. After the openings are cut out, the result looks like large-scale lace. The lace is then fused to the outline fabric to provide a firm framework over which the edges of the window openings are turned.

1. To temporarily adhere the freezer paper to the interfacing, place the **shiny side** of the freezer paper on top of the **non-glue side** of the fusible interfacing. Lightly iron the 2 layers using a low to medium setting. Although it seems that the fusible interfacing will permanently bond to the ironing surface, if you work quickly the interfacing will gently pull away from the surface without leaving a residue.

Note: *I don't recommend the use of a Teflon pressing sheet because I've found the glue dots from the interfacing come off and stick to the pressing sheet permanently. Remember that it is not necessary to iron for a long time to get the freezer paper and interfacing to hold together.*

If the design on the freezer paper is larger than the interfacing, overlap and stitch 2 pieces of interfacing together to make one large piece.

Lace Practice

Use this exercise to practice cutting through the layers of freezer paper and fusible interfacing with a craft knife. Make sure you are comfortable cutting smooth curves and sharp points before you begin your quilt.

MATERIALS

2 pieces of 5" x 5" freezer paper
2 pieces of 5" x 5" medium-weight fusible interfacing
Pencil
Iron
Craft knife
Cutting mat

EXERCISE

1. Trace each shape onto the dull side of the freezer paper with a pencil.
2. Iron the shiny side of the freezer paper to the non-glue side of the fusible interfacing.
3. Cut out each shape carefully.

Practice these steps until you can cut smooth curves and sharp points.

2. To create the lace, place the layered freezer paper and fusible interfacing on a cutting mat. Hold the craft knife like a pencil and cut out the windows, leaving the outlines intact and connected. The lace should remain in one piece. Press firmly enough to cut through both layers. If you cannot easily remove a piece that you've cut, you may have a dull blade or you may not be pressing firmly enough. Be careful not to cut beyond the drawn lines or beyond the inner points.

Cut through both layers with a craft knife.

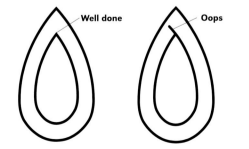

Do not cut beyond the drawn lines or the inner points.

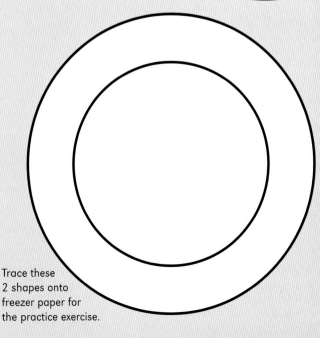

Trace these 2 shapes onto freezer paper for the practice exercise.

PREPARE THE OUTLINE

The outline fabric frames the cutout windows. Choose the outline fabric carefully. You will get a very different look depending on the value and color of the outline fabric. (Use the Color Practice on page 17 to see how an outline fabric will affect your other color choices.)

The outline fabric affects the overall feeling of the quilt.

1. Carefully place the *fusible* side of the lace onto the *wrong* side of the outline fabric. Smooth out any wrinkles. The lace can be tricky to handle, so do not remove the freezer paper yet. Take your time to make sure that the lace is smooth and not twisted or distorted.

2. Fuse the lace to the outline fabric, long enough to tack it in place. Once it is tacked, turn the entire piece over and following the fusing instructions for the interfacing you are using. I've found that if you iron too long on the freezer

paper, it's very difficult to remove. If you iron on the reverse side, the freezer paper is easier to remove.

Tack the lace in place with the iron, then turn the piece over and fuse completely.

3. After the fabric is cool, carefully remove the freezer paper. Some fusible interfacings release better than others do. It's a good idea to test your interfacing with freezer paper before starting a project.

> If the freezer paper is difficult to remove from the interfacing, crumple the entire piece or soak it in water to help the paper release.

The surface is ready.

The outline fabric surface for your quilt is now ready. You can begin to do Subtractive Appliqué.

Subtractive Appliqué

Windows are the areas you cut open within the piece; the outline fabric acts as a frame around the colored fabrics that you insert in the windows. The most revealing moment in developing a quilt comes when you subtract the excess outline fabric and begin to add color. The quilt comes to life as you experiment with fabrics and their placement.

It is time to begin subtracting the excess fabric and allow the design to emerge.

CREATE WINDOWS

1. To create windows, use a scissors to cut out the interior of 3 or 4 interfaced areas, leaving a $^3/_{16}$" turn-under allowance. Be sure to select windows that don't touch each other—this makes it easier to add and sew

the colored fabric. If you cut more than a few of these windows at one time the piece will distort and be difficult to manage.

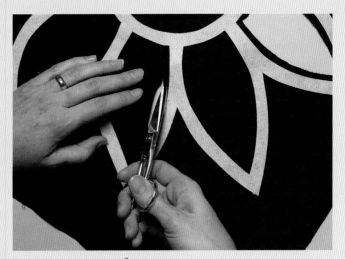

Cut windows leaving a $^3/_{16}$" allowance.

Cut only a few windows at a time. Finish the Subtractive Appliqué process for these windows before cutting more. This will keep distortion of the piece to a minimum.

2. Clip the concave curves and points. Notch the convex curves. This will ensure smoothly turned edges. Be careful not to cut past the $^3/_{16}$" allowance into the interfacing.

Clip the concave curves.   Notch the convex curves.

3. Generously spray-starch the edges of the cutout outline fabric to saturate the turn-under allowances. The starch loosens the fibers to allow the seams to turn easily. It also helps hold them in place after pressing.

4. While the window shape is wet with starch, carefully fold the turn-under allowance onto the interfacing, using the interfacing as a guide. Make sure to ease the allowances around curves and points accurately. Press until completely dry, using a mini iron on the *medium* setting. A dry, starched, and pressed seam will stay in place.

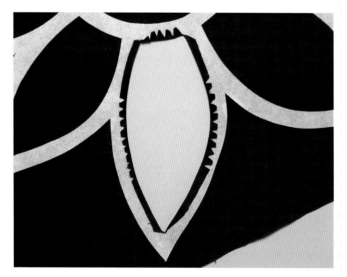

Fold and turn the allowances onto the interfacing.

Pressing is important. Use a mini iron to ease shoulder and neck tension.

CUT AND INSERT WINDOW FABRIC

You may want to color code the windows on your design before beginning. This will prevent you from inserting the wrong fabric into a window. Color-coding can be done many ways. You might assign each fabric a number and write that number in all of its windows on your small-scale paper copy of the design. You can also color the design using your computer or use colored pencils on the design paper. You are cutting and filling windows that don't touch each other, so having a plan on paper will prevent mistakes.

1. Place the window fabric *wrong side up*. On top of this, place the outline fabric *wrong side up*. Trace the cut out window shape onto the *wrong side* of the colored fabric. Remove the window fabric from underneath the outline fabric and add a $^1/_2$" allowance around the entire traced shape. Cut out with scissors.

Trace the inside of the window shape onto the **wrong side** of the colored fabric.

2. After you cut colored fabrics for the prepared windows, place the right side of the window fabric onto the wrong side (interfaced side) of the outline fabric. Glue or pin the fabric in place. If you use glue, press the fabrics together firmly so the pieces attach together securely. Don't worry about using a glue stick; it's safe to use on fabric and it won't come off on your machine or needle when completely dry.

Glue or pin the colored fabric in the window.

Sometimes inserting larger pieces of fabric in the windows can be quite a challenge. *Into My Garden* (see page 56) had many of these troublesome pieces. Larger pieces of window fabric often have bias edges that can be difficult to work with. To prevent distortion, make sure the window fabric and the outline fabric are completely smooth, then both glue and pin all around the window piece to secure it in place before stitching.

> *When working with bias edges, it is best to use both glue and pins along the edges. Using both prevents wrinkles and/or distortion in the quilt.*

APPLIQUÉ

When you are ready to stitch, turn the piece over to the right side. Check the windows to make sure they are neatly turned. Carefully examine all the points and curves. The curves should be free from dents and bumps. Threads at the interior and exterior points should be tucked under. No loose threads from the fabric should show on the quilt top.

1. Thread the sewing machine with monofilament thread in the top. Fill the bobbin with thread to match the outline fabric. Test the sewing machine's zigzag stitch on a sample appliqué. Make sure to adjust the thread tension appropriately so that the bobbin thread doesn't show on the quilt top. You may need to decrease the stitch width and length slightly so the stitches are less visible. Careful attention to the tension, stitch width, and stitch length will result in beautiful stitches.

The bobbin thread (in red) appears on the top when the thread tension is incorrect.

> *Thread tension is important for a clean zigzag stitch. Always make a test sample using the same materials in your quilt to determine the best combination of settings for your sewing machine. These samples can also be used to make sure the iron temperature is set properly for monofilament thread.*

Practice

Appliqué Practice

Use this exercise to practice turning and appliquéing difficult shapes before starting a larger project. Now is a good time to perfect turning, experiment with thread tension, and practice the zigzag stitch.

MATERIALS
Black fabric
Colored fabric
Freezer paper
Fusible interfacing
Monofilament thread
Dark bobbin thread
Glue stick
Scissors
Pencil

EXERCISE

1. Trace the 2 shapes from the Lace Practice exercise on page 25 onto the dull side of freezer paper.

2. Follow the instructions on pages 24–26 to iron the freezer paper onto the fusible interfacing, cut out the lace, and fuse the lace to the black outline fabric.

3. Cut out the openings of the windows and turn under the allowances as described on pages 27–28. Remember to notch and clip where necessary.

4. Cut and insert the fabrics into the windows as described on pages 28–29.

5. Appliqué the shapes, finding the best machine settings for neat, clean stitches.

6. Record your machine settings here:
Stitch length: _____
Stitch width: _____
Top tension: _____
Needle type and size: _____
Thread type and size: _____

2. Once the tension is correctly set, with the piece right side up, zigzag over the outline and window fabrics, catching both fabrics. Make sure to backstitch a few stitches at the beginning and end of each shape to lock the stitching.

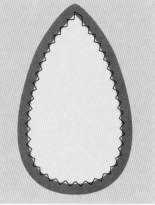

Zigzag over the outline and window fabrics, catching both fabrics.

3. After the shapes have been stitched, press from the front side with the iron on a medium setting. Remember, monofilament thread will melt if it is ironed at a high setting, so it's a good idea to test the iron temperature on a stitched sample to make sure the iron is not too hot.

4. The contrasting colored fabrics inserted into the windows are cut larger than the window. To reduce bulk, trim away the excess fabric on the wrong side approximately $1/8$" from the stitching. This prevents the quilt from becoming too stiff and eases stitching of future windows.

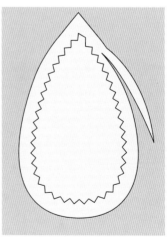

Trim away the excess fabric $1/8$" from the stitching.

5. Repeat the Create Windows, Cut and Insert Window Fabric, and Appliqué sequences (pages 27–29) with 3 or 4 windows at a time, until the quilt top is complete.

Add Borders

The decision of whether or not to add a border is often quite intuitive. I like to add a border to enrich the quilt with color and to generate more interest or movement in the piece. The border also frames the quilt.

SQUARE UP THE TOP

When the appliqué is finished, you'll find that the quilt is not square. Many pieces stick out from the sides and need to be trimmed off.

1. Before you square up your quilt top, you need to determine the size to trim it to. Find the size by adding $^1/_2$" to the original planned size; this allows a $^1/_4$" seam allowance on all sides. For instance, if the design is 30" x 40", measure and cut the top to $30^1/_2$" x $40^1/_2$". Use a cutting mat, ruler, and rotary cutter to cut away the excess fabric. Approach this cautiously and make sure not to cut away too much. Also, use a large rectangular or square rotary cutting ruler to make sure the corners are cut to a true 90° angle.

Cut away the excess to square up the quilt top.

INNER BORDER

An inner border sets the center image apart from a pieced border. I prefer to use the outline fabric to make a thin inner border between the quilt and the pieced border.

1. To make an inner border, cut 1"-wide strips that are at least 1" longer than the corresponding edges of the quilt.

2. Sew the inner border to the longer sides to the quilt first.

3. Trim away the excess even with the quilt edge.

4. Press the seams open.

5. Repeat with the remaining sides of the quilt.

PIECED BORDERS

Many of my recent quilts contain a pieced border. They are the result of a happy accident. As I worked on *Butterflies* (see page 51), I realized near the end of the project that I had forgotten to add red-violet into the composition as planned. I experimented with various-sized squares and borders. I decided to use a 6"-wide pieced border with 1" x 1" assorted squares to bring in the red-violet fabric, and to achieve a sense of movement in the border. For this composition, 2" x 2" squares were too distracting to the eye and, mathematically, $1^1/2$" x $1^1/2$" squares didn't fit.

Prepare the Border

To prepare for a pieced border, you need to estimate how much fabric you need based on the finished size of the quilt and width of the border. I like to use 1" x 1" (finished size) squares, rather than larger squares. The smaller squares keep the eyes from focusing too much on the border, and allow them to move around the entire piece. It is also very easy to determine how many squares you need when they are 1" x 1".

1. Determine the finished size of the quilt with the border. For example, if the quilt is 30" x 20" without a border, a 2"-wide border adds 2" to each side. The final finished size of the quilt will measure 30" + 2" + 2", which is 34" in width, and 20" + 2" + 2", which is 24" in length.

2. Determine the number of 1" x 1" finished squares needed for your border width by subtracting the inner area of the quilt without the border (inner length without the border x inner width without the border) from the total area of the quilt (finished length x finished width).

Continuing with the example:

Total Area: 24" x 34" = 816

Inner Area: 20" x 30" = 600

Number of 1" x 1" finished squares = 816 - 600 = 216

Close-up of *Butterflies* border

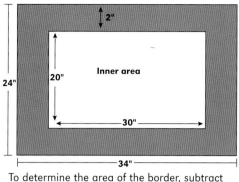

To determine the area of the border, subtract the inner area from the total area.

3. You now can estimate how many $1^1/_2$"-wide strips of fabric you need to cut to make strip sets for the 1" x 1" finished squares. One $1^1/_2$" strip of 40"-wide fabric yields approximately 25 of these small squares. Divide the number of squares needed by 25, then round up to the nearest whole number that is evenly divisible by the border width.

The key to figuring the yardage is that the number of strips needed for the strip sets is always a multiple of the width of the border because of the way the strips are sewn together. If the border is 2" wide, the number of strips needed must be evenly divisible by 2. If the border is 5" wide, the number of strips needed must be evenly divisible by 5.

4. To finish the example:
To make the 216 squares: 216 ÷ 25 = 8.64. Round up to the nearest whole number *and* because the border is 2"-wide, you will need 10 strips of fabric because 10 is the next number that is evenly divisible by 2.

Cut and Sew the Border

Select a range of border fabrics you think will complement the piece. Use the practice exercise to create a test block. Notice that in *Good Morning* (see page 58) I used blues and greens to complement the yellow background, yet in *Welcome* (see page 54) I used yellows to repeat and enhance the yellow of the pineapple.

1. Cut the strips for the pieced border using a rotary cutter, ruler, and mat. For 1" x 1" finished squares, cut border strips $1^1/_2$" x the width of the fabric. (See Prepare the Border on page 29 to determine how many strips to cut.)

2. After you cut the strips from the variety of border fabrics, thread the sewing machine (top and bobbin thread) with thread that matches the fabric strips. Use a $^1/_4$" seam allowance to sew the strips together lengthwise in random order so that no similar fabrics touch each other. Press all seams to one side. The number of strips in a strip set is equal to the number of inches in the finished width of the border. For example, if you want a 2"-wide border, sew sets of 2 strips. If you want a 5"-wide border, sew sets of 5 strips. Vary fabrics and their position in each strip set to help achieve randomness in the finished border. The finished strip set should measure $^1/_2$" larger in width than the desired border width.

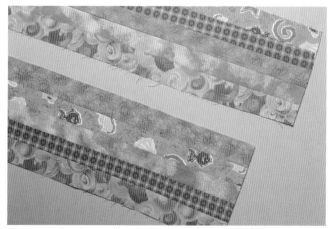

Sew sets of strips together.

Press the strip sets carefully with an up and down motion. The strips are long and easy to distort if you iron with a back and forth motion.

Practice

Border Practice

Use this exercise to view a sample border before you begin sewing.

MATERIALS

A variety of fabrics in a range of values from one
    color family
White scratch paper
Glue stick
Rotary cutter, ruler, and mat

EXERCISE

1. Cut a total of 25 squares 1" x 1" from the selected fabrics.

2. Glue the squares to the scratch paper to form a 5" x 5" square.

3. Cut out the finished border sample (5" x 5").

4. Place the border sample next to the quilt top. Ask yourself the following questions:

- Does the border sample complement or distract from the composition?
- Is it too busy or too flat?
- Does the quilt look better with or without the border sample?

If you do not like the sample you have made, make another sample from a different selection of fabrics. Be sure to save these samples, they may give you ideas for other quilts.

Pieced border sample

3. Place the strip set right side up on a cutting mat and cut into 1¹/₂" units. Check regularly to make sure the edges and seams align with the ruler markings. You may need to square up the strip set after every few cuts.

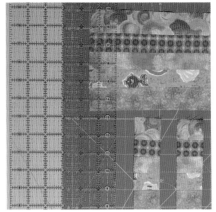

Cut 1¹/₂" units.

4. Sew the 1¹/₂" units together with a ¹/₄" seam allowance to form border strip lengths that correspond to the dimensions of the quilt. Make sure seams are aligned from one unit to the next by carefully pinning.

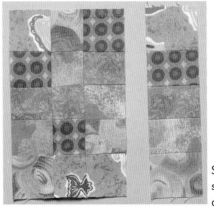

Sew 1¹/₂" units together so that no similar fabrics are touching.

5. Press the seams open.

6. Sew the border strips to the long sides of the quilt top first. Press the seams open.

7. Repeat with the short sides of the quilt top.

FINISH THE TOP

1. When the quilt top is assembled, press it using an iron on a medium setting. As before, make sure the iron is not too hot for the monofilament thread. Be careful not to stretch the seams in the border.

2. Square up the quilt, using the method described on page 40.

Quilt to Add Movement

Texture and quilting distinguish a quilt. You can achieve texture in a variety of ways. For instance, I've seen quilts textured with beads, buttons, and even CDs. I choose to stitch simple lines to create texture and a sense of movement.

How can simple lines create movement? It's easy. You can stitch lines that tell a story or lead the eyes to move across the quilt. Lines can even soothe or create tension. In the quilt *Opening Day*, I've sewn lines that suggest waves in the ocean. They accompany the sailing theme and make the eyes glide across the piece following the quilted waves.

In *Opening Day* the quilting suggests the ocean waves.

Often, when it's time to quilt a piece, it's easy to become rushed to finish the quilt. You'll find that when you quilt for movement, you will be able to set a design and quilt it quite quickly. Try not to focus too long on what design to sew into the piece; let the natural lines direct you. Although there are many ways of quilting a quilt, I almost always stitch channels of parallel lines. I usually make an intuitive decision based on the lines in the quilt and the movement I want to accentuate. Then I draw one line as a guide and use it as a reference to quilt the entire piece.

Prepare to Quilt

Before you quilt, you will need to prepare the quilt top.

1. Make sure the quilt top is pressed, trimmed, and squared to the appropriate size (see page 31).

2. Cut the backing and batting at least 4" larger than the top.

3. Layer the backing fabric, batting, and top respectively. Use the basting method you prefer and baste the layers together.

Layer the backing, batting, and top.

Draw One Line

The first drawn line sets the tone for movement. Use this critical line to focus on an element or to divide the quilt. Look for a single element in the quilt design that draws the attention. Use this element as a guide for the first line. Draw this first line on the quilt with an erasable pen or chalk pencil.

Try not to draw straight vertical or horizontal lines for quilting. They are difficult to repeat perfectly throughout the piece.

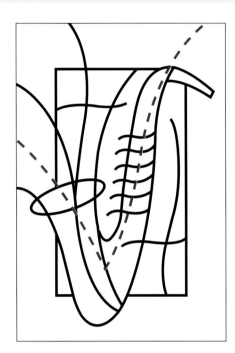

Draw the first line.

Sometimes I draw an additional line or two to quilt if I want greater detail in the quilting. For example, in *Mothers Day III*, I stitched circular centers around each flower. I stitched lines that radiate from the center, to give the piece a sense of energy.

In *Mothers Day III* the circular stitches around the flower add energy.

Practice

Quilting Practice

Use this exercise to practice creating movement. Use a prominent element of the drawing to guide the first drawn line. Draw successive lines to create movement.

MATERIALS
Paper and pencil

EXERCISE

1. Make several copies of the provided drawings, enlarging them if you like. On each drawing, use a pencil to draw a single line that focuses on a prominent element. Look at the quilts in the Gallery (pages 43–60) for ideas.
2. Draw successive parallel lines and see how they create movement.
3. Make more copies of the drawings and repeat this exercise. Try different first lines to achieve varying effects. Focus on other prominent elements for guiding your first drawn line and see what effect it has.

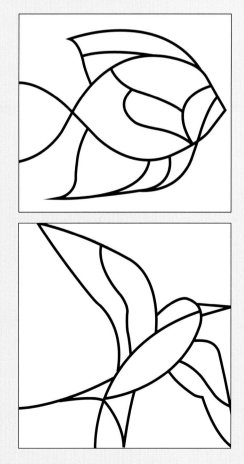

QUILT

1. After you draw the first line on the quilt, you can quilt it. Use a walking foot with a moveable guide for the quilting. The walking foot feeds the three layers of the quilt through the sewing machine evenly. This prevents puckers on the reverse side of the quilt. The guide follows the previously stitched line and leads you to quilt consistent parallel lines.

The walking foot and guide

2. For quilting that stands out, use a heavyweight thread, such as buttonhole or topstitching thread, on the top. In the bobbin use a regular weight thread that matches the top thread. Be sure to use a needle that is appropriate for the size of the thread. I use a universal 90/12 for heavyweight thread. Next, lengthen the stitch to compensate for the heavier weight of thread and the thickness of the quilt. Sometimes, you need to adjust the top tension as well. Make a test sample and experiment with the stitch length and tension until you achieve beautiful stitches.

Heavyweight buttonhole thread for quilting   **Regular weight thread for bobbin**

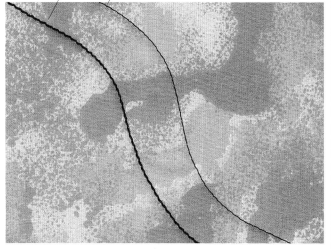

Use heavyweight thread for quilting that stands out.

3. Now that your machine is set to quilt, stitch slowly and evenly on the drawn line. Next, quilt successive parallel lines. The guide on the walking foot helps you quilt the succeeding lines quickly and naturally. Line up the guide approximately $1/2"$–$5/8"$ away from the first line. If you do not have a guide, you can estimate a $1/8"$–$1/4"$ gap between the edge of the walking foot and the previous stitched line for the next stitched line. I aim for consistent parallel lines. This requires balance between quilting speed and steady control. Stitch lines until you have reached the edge of the quilt or finished quilting a specific area.

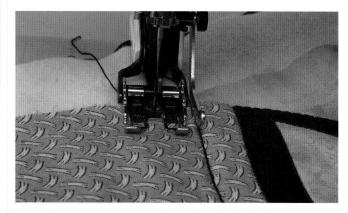

To stitch parallel lines, line up the guide with the first line.

It's easy to get discouraged when the lines don't look perfect close-up. If this occurs, put the quilt on the design wall and view it from a few steps away. With all the other quilting and design in the piece, you will not see the imperfections— you will only see the overall impact.

Finish the Quilt

BLOCK THE QUILT

A blocked quilt keeps its shape and hangs square and flat.

1. If the quilting distorted the piece, gently smooth it on a large flat surface. I like to work on a piece of heavyweight cardboard on top of my carpet—gridded cardboard is my favorite (available where sewing and dressmaking supplies are sold). By placing the quilt on the gridded cardboard, I can measure and verify that the quilt is square and even. Insert pins through the quilt directly into the cardboard around the perimeter of the quilt. Make sure that the opposite edges of the quilt top are parallel to each other.

Also, be careful not to stretch one side longer than the other side. The two sides should be the same length, and the top and bottom edges should be the same length.

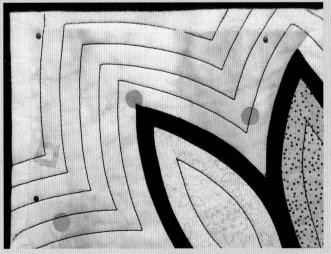

Insert pins through the quilt into the cardboard.

2. Use an iron on its highest steam setting to steam the quilt top. Hold the iron just above the quilt surface while the iron produces steam. Do not touch the quilt surface with the hot iron: you will melt the monofilament thread and flatten the quilted texture. If the iron doesn't produce enough steam, mist the quilt with water in a spray bottle.

Hold the iron just above the quilt surface while the iron produces steam, being careful not to melt the monofilament thread.

3. Allow the quilt to dry while pinned in place. Remove the pins when the quilt is completely dry. Don't rush the drying process. In some climates, it can take from several hours to several days for the quilt top to dry completely.

SQUARE UP THE QUILT

After you block the quilt, it should be flat and ready to square up.

1. To square up the quilt, use a ruler to trim away the excess batting and backing, leaving $1/4$" beyond all sides of the quilt top. This will leave enough for a $1/2$"-wide finished binding.

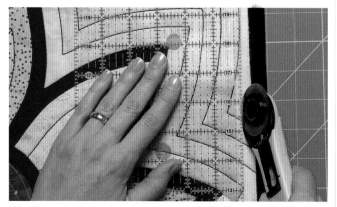

Trim away the excess batting and backing $1/4$" beyond all sides of the quilt top.

2. Use a T-square or ruler to make sure the corners are a perfect 90° angle. Measure each side and make sure to trim the quilt so that the opposite sides are parallel and equal in length and that the corners are square.

BIND THE QUILT

I use a $1/2$"-wide (finished) double-fold continuous binding with mitered corners. I like my binding to be the same width as the spacing width of my quilted lines. This makes the binding fade visually and blend into the entire piece.

1. Before you cut the binding, measure the perimeter of the quilt and add 12" to the measurement.

2. To make a $1/2$"-wide binding that is consistent with the suggested quilted line spacing, cut the binding fabric either on the bias or on the straight of grain, in $2^3/4$"-wide strips. Cut enough strips so that when you join them to make one continuous strip, they fit around the perimeter of the quilt plus 12".

> *Binding made by cutting the fabric on the bias is stronger. It will hold up to wear and tear longer than a binding on the straight of grain. It also goes more smoothly around curves and folds nicely for mitered corners.*

3. Sew the strips together with diagonal seams to make one continuous strip. Press seams open.

4. Fold the binding in half lengthwise, with the right sides out. Press.

5. Place the binding around the quilt top to make sure you have enough. Make sure the joined seams of the strips do not fall on a corner. If they are on a corner, the miter will be bulky and difficult to fold. Continue to test-fit the binding until you are pleased with the position.

6. Line up the raw edge of the binding with the edge of the quilt top. Pin the binding in place.

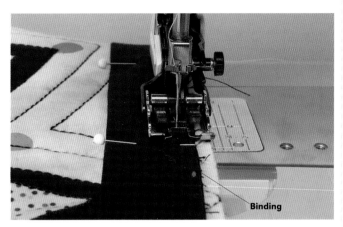

Line up the raw edge of the binding to the raw edge of the quilt top. Stitch using a $^1/4$" seam allowance.

7. Leave about 6" of binding free at the beginning. Then, use a $^1/4$" seam allowance, and stitch the binding to the quilt until you reach $^1/4$" from a corner edge of the quilt top. Use a walking foot to prevent the binding from stretching unevenly.

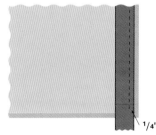

Stitch to $^1/4$" from corner.

8. Pivot the quilt and fold the binding away from the quilt. This forms a 45° fold line.

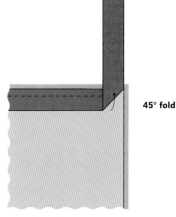

First fold for miter

9. Next, fold the binding down against the quilt edge, lining up the edges. Begin stitching $^1/4$" from the corner edge. Repeat this process around the quilt edge and at each corner.

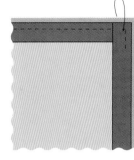

Second fold alignment

When using a walking foot, adjust your needle position for a $^1/4$" seam so the edge of the foot can line up with the edge of the binding. You can also use a seam guide on the throat plate of the sewing machine to give you a $^1/2$" seam from the needle to the edge of the backing/batting.

10. When you finish all the corners and get within 6" of the binding end, stop sewing with the needle down in the fabric. Fold the beginning free end of the binding under $^1/2$", finger-pressing it. Next, tuck a few inches of the other end inside the beginning end, trimming if necessary. Pin in place. This joins the ends of the binding and you can then continue to sew this to the quilt. When done attaching the binding to the quilt, blindstitch the folded binding end to the end that you tucked inside.

11. Fold the binding over to the back of the quilt. Pin the binding in place. Hand stitch the binding to the backside of the quilt with a slip stitch. Make sure the stitches do not come through to the front of the quilt. Take care to fold down the mitered corners and stitch them.

ATTACH A SLEEVE

If you want to hang the quilt, attach a sleeve to the backside. Try to match the sleeve fabric to the backing of the quilt.

1. To make a sleeve, cut a strip of fabric 7$1/2$"-wide by the width of the quilt.

2. Fold the short ends of the sleeve under $1/4$" twice and press.

3. Stitch along each folded edge. Fold the sleeve in half lengthwise with the right sides together. Stitch a $1/4$" seam along the length. Press the seam open.

4. Turn the sleeve right side out. Press the sleeve flat with the long seam centered on one side.

5. Center the sleeve on the quilt back and align one long edge of the sleeve $1/4$" away from the binding. Secure the top and the bottom of the sleeve with pins. Slipstitch the top and bottom of the sleeve to the quilt, making sure the stitches catch only the backing fabric.

FINAL BLOCKING

Sometimes a quilt becomes wavy after you attach the binding and sleeve. To eliminate any distortion, block the quilt a second time.

1. Gently smooth the quilt on a large flat surface covered with cardboard.

2. Insert pins through the quilt top, *not the binding*, directly into the cardboard around the perimeter of the quilt. If you insert pins into the binding, it tends to distort the quilt more and dent the binding.

3. As before, the two sides should be the same length, the top and bottom edges should measure the same, and the opposite sides should be parallel.

4. Follow the instructions in Block the Quilt (pages 39–40) to complete the final blocking of the quilt.

GALLERY

AMERICAN CAFÉ

30" x 24", 2002, private collection.

When I returned home to the states after traveling
on business in Europe, I was surprised and quickly
reminded that our coffee cups are much larger than
those in Europe.

RED

30" x 24", 2002, private collection.

This quilt celebrates California wines. I included my
own mono-printed, screen-printed, dyed, painted, and
foiled fabrics. A pieced border surrounds the quilt.

FIELD OF FLOWERS

55" x 55", 2003.

I loved the empty field near my childhood home
that was filled with sunflowers each year. I recalled
this memory in this quilt that uses my hand-dyed
pink fabrics stamped with silver foil and painted
swirls in the centers of the sunflowers. I used a
black-and-white checkerboard border whose playful
nature reminds me of childhood.

SWEET SEPTEMBER

18" x 18", 2003.

Last year a few friends and I ventured up to Apple Hill, where we collected apples, ate pies, and drank cider. This quilt commemorates that occasion. The bowl is made from pieced fabrics.

LAZY DAISY

18" x 18", 2002, private collection.

The use of contrasting background and foreground colors gives this *Lazy Daisy* some pizzazz. Notice that in even the smallest quilts, I use a variety of fabrics and values.

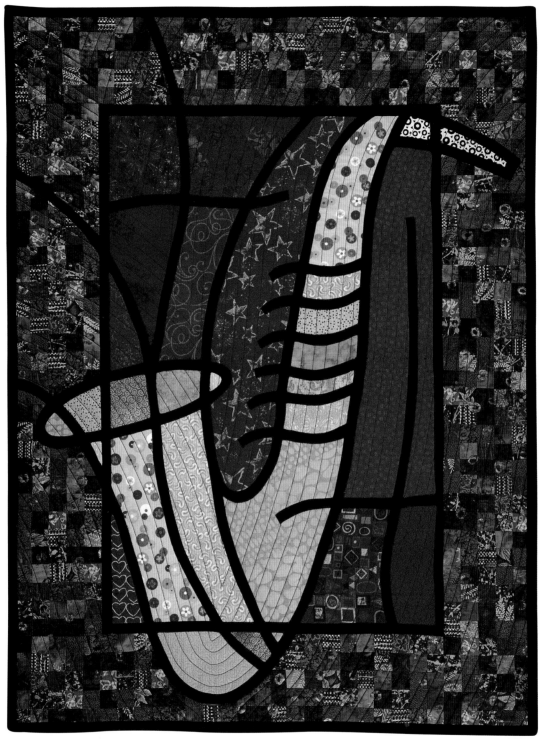

JAZZ IT UP

30" x 40", 2002.

In our city, the annual jazz jubilee has everyone dancing. The pieced border of this quilt is embellished with screen-printed foil circles.

MARTINI LUNCH

30" x 24", 2002, private collection.

Lunch with the ladies in the high-tech industry was
always fun. An occasional martini made it memo-
rable, and this quilt shares the memories.

DRAGONFLY

18" x 18", 2001, private collection.
The dragonfly design was the
beginning of a new series of quilts.

Photo by Bob Perrin

DRAGONFLY II

18" x 18", 2002, private collection.

In this quilt, I have designed and screen-printed a mosaic

on the background fabrics to suggest broken tiles. This quilt

is a color and fabric variation of the original *Dragonfly*.

BUTTERFLIES

45" x 35", 2002, private collection.

I don't get to garden regularly anymore. In my longing
to garden, I brought butterflies back into my life with
the creation of this piece. It was a breakthrough piece
for me. I successfully created a design that extended
beyond the inner edging onto the pieced border.

FISHES

30" x 41", 2002, private collection.

I saw beautiful and colorful fish while snorkeling. I created
this quilt to suggest their vibrancy and the clarity of the
water. I couldn't find the perfect, commercial, shimmery
water fabric to include in this quilt, so I hand dyed, painted,
stamped, and foiled the yellow-green background fabric.

OPENING DAY

28" x 29", 2003, private collection.

I wanted to create the serene feeling that I experience when I watch sailboats in the San Francisco Bay. To create a sense of peacefulness, I needed calming colors. After I experimented with the design on the computer, I changed the black lines to white. With this change, the piece became more serene. In this quilt, I used a combination of hand-dyed, painted, and commercial fabrics. I included a pieced border to further the calm feeling.

SHAPES AND SIZES

40" x 30", 2003, private collection.

People are all shapes, sizes, and colors; yet a common thread joins us. I used a single quilted line stitched in a maze to show how we are all connected even though we are different. Many of the fabrics are foiled and printed.

WELCOME

18" x 24", 2002, private collection.
The pineapple is a common symbol for
hospitality in Hawaiian culture. It welcomes
guests into the home. For added texture in
the pineapple fruit, I used a traditional
diamond piecing technique.

TWO

18" x 18", 2003.
Two cups of coffee and high tea at
2:00 p.m. were the inspiration for this
piece. The cups are commercial fabrics
that I over-painted with a light pink.

REUBEN

30" x 40", 2002.

In the quaint town of Fair Oaks, California, roosters and chickens roam freely. My husband and I were married at a small historic home in that town. *Reuben* pays tribute to the rooster who stood on the roof watching and singing to my husband and me while we exchanged our wedding vows.

INTO MY GARDEN

50" x 50", 2002.

I used to spend a lot of time in my garden. I planted a
variety of roses, bulbs, and seasonal flowers to color the
backyard. Now, because I spend all of my time with my
family and making quilts, my garden has become quite
overgrown and unruly, as this quilt depicts. This was my
first experiment with a pieced border.

MOTHERS DAY I Photo by Bob Perrin
24" x 30" 2001, private collection.

MOTHERS DAY II Photo by Bob Perrin
24" x 30" 2001, private collection.

MOTHERS DAY III
28" x 34", 2001.
Flowers are such a joy to give
and to receive. In reverence of
mothers, I created this series of
three flowerpot quilts.

GOOD MORNING

40" x 30", 2002.

When I visit a favorite vacation spot in Hawaii, there are
many wonderful plumeria trees. Their morning fragrance
is sweet and unforgettable. Inspired by these times, I
always think what a "good morning" it is to be able to
pick a plumeria and put it in my hair. *Good Morning* cap-
tures this moment with the cool refreshing border of
blues, the warm sunny background, and the fresh white
flowers with painted centers.

LAUREL CROWN

36" x 36", 2002.

This is the second of my complex Four-Patch quilts. I used a variety of my hand-dyed, printed, and painted fabrics to complement the commercial fabrics.

REMEMBERING SUMMER

18" x 24", 2002, private collection.

This piece for a client celebrates the summer and all its blooms.

FOUR PATCH EVOLUTION

36" x 36", 2002, private collection.

This quilt is both an evolution of the standard Four-Patch quilt, and an evolution in my work. This complex Four-Patch is a four-way mirror image of a dragonfly design. It uses a simple black-and-white palette with accents of red and hand-stamped gold-foil squares.

UPSTREAM

38" x 29", 2003.

I revisited a black-and-white theme with this companion to *Four Patch Evolution*. Again, I created hand-stamped gold-foil squares on the ivory fabric to glisten against the solid black fabric.

PROJECTS

Leaves

Finished quilt size: 24" x 30"

Bring nature inside with these *Leaves*. This is a good project to get you started. The shapes are easy to handle and the color palette is limited, making fabric selection easy. Observe the color changes and values of the leaves outside your home. Be sure to use a variety of values and patterns in your quilt. For the background, use a variety of fabrics within a family of closely related colors that contrast with the leaves.

MATERIALS

See page 7 for complete descriptions of tools and supplies.

Black or dark colored fabric for outline and binding:
   $1^1/_4$ yards

Pink, orange, and yellow-orange fabrics for background:
   a variety to total $^2/_3$ yard

Green and yellow-green fabrics for leaves: a variety to
   total $^1/_2$ yard

Batting: 28" x 34"

Backing: 1 yard

Freezer paper: $1^1/_2$ yards of 18"-wide

Medium-weight fusible interfacing: $1^1/_2$ yards of 22"-wide

Monofilament thread

Black sewing thread for the bobbin

Thread for quilting

Glue stick

Pins

Scissors for trimming fabric

Craft knife

Rotary cutter, ruler, and mat

CUTTING

Black or dark colored fabric for outline: Cut 1 rectangle
   25" x 31".

Black or dark colored fabric for binding: Cut 3 strips
   $2^3/_4$" wide x width of fabric.

Freezer paper: Cut 2 pieces 18" x 26".

Fusible interfacing: Cut 2 pieces 22" x 26".

PREPARATION

*See pages 22–26 for complete instructions on how to
enlarge, trace, and create the lace.*

1. Slightly overlap the 2 pieces of freezer paper lengthwise. Secure them with transparent tape on the dull side
to form 1 piece that measures approximately 35" x 26".
Trim to 32" x 26".

2. Slightly overlap the 2 pieces of fusible interfacing
lengthwise. Stitch them together to form 1 piece that
measures approximately 43" x 26". You may want to cut
this piece to 32" x 26" so it is the same size as the freezer paper. This will be $^1/_2$" larger on all sides than the
outline fabric.

3. Use your favorite method to enlarge the pattern on
page 64 by 320%. Note that this pattern is already
reversed for tracing.

4. Trace the enlarged pattern onto the dull side of the
freezer paper.

5. To temporarily attach the freezer paper to the interfacing, lightly iron the *shiny* side of the freezer paper to
the *non-glue* side of the fusible interfacing.

6. Use a craft knife to cut through the freezer paper and
the fusible interfacing to form the lace.

7. Fuse the lace onto the wrong side of the outline fabric.

8. Remove the freezer paper.

APPLIQUÉ

*See pages 27–30 for complete instructions on how to
create the windows and appliqué.*

1. Cut out a few windows at a time leaving a $^3/_{16}$" turn-
under allowance. Make sure the windows are not next
to each other.

2. Clip as needed, turn and press the window edges to
the interfaced side.

3. Insert and glue or pin the window fabrics in place.

4. Use the monofilament thread on top and the black
thread in the bobbin. Zigzag on the right side of the
quilt top, catching both the window and outline fabrics.
Backstitch at the beginning and end to anchor the stitches.

5. Press with an iron on a medium setting. Monofilament
thread melts at high settings.

6. Repeat, doing 3 or 4 windows at a time, until the quilt
top is complete.

FINISHING

*See pages 35–42 for complete instructions on quilting
and finishing techniques.*

Trim, quilt, and bind the piece. Block the quilt, if desired.

Leaves

Enlarge 320%.

Pattern is already reversed for tracing.

Go Fishing

Finished quilt size: 33" x 41"

Capture the movement of the sea as you *Go Fishing*. The light-colored outline fabric gives this quilt a brightness that recalls the sun reflecting on the water. A range of light blue-greens and blues for the background will suggest calm, shimmery waters and contrast nicely with the white outlines. Have fun finding fabrics that convey a watery theme, such as bubbles and waves.

MATERIALS

See page 7 for complete descriptions of tools and supplies.

White or light colored fabric for outline and binding:
$1^5/_8$ yards

Light blue and blue-green fabrics for background water:
a variety to total $1^1/_2$ yards

Orange and red-orange prints for first fish: a variety to
total $^1/_4$ yard

Yellow prints for second fish: a variety to total $^1/_4$ yard

Pink and pink-orange prints for third fish: a variety to
total $^1/_4$ yard

Black-and-white prints for fish accents: a variety to total
$^1/_4$ yard

Black fabric and white fabric for the fish eyes: 1 scrap
of each at least 4" x 4"

Batting: 37" x 45"

Backing: $1^1/_4$ yards

Freezer paper: $2^1/_2$ yards of 18"-wide

Medium-weight fusible interfacing: $2^1/_2$ yards of 22"-wide

Paper-backed fusible web: 8" x 4"

Monofilament thread

White sewing thread for the bobbin

Thread for quilting

Glue stick

Pins

Scissors for trimming fabric

Craft knife

Rotary cutter, ruler, and mat

CUTTING

White or light colored fabric for outline: Cut 1 rectangle
34" x 42".

White or light colored fabric for binding: Cut 4 strips
$2^3/_4$" wide x width of fabric.

Black fabric: Cut 1 square 4" x 4" for the eyes.

White fabric: Cut 1 square 4" x 4" for the eyes.

Paper-backed fusible web: Cut 2 squares 4" x 4".

Freezer paper: Cut 2 pieces 18" x 43".

Fusible interfacing: Cut 2 pieces 22" x 43".

PREPARATION

*See pages 22–26 for complete instructions on how to
enlarge, trace, and create the lace.*

1. Slightly overlap the 2 pieces of freezer paper lengthwise. Secure them with transparent tape on the dull side
to form 1 piece that measures approximately 35" x 43".

2. Slightly overlap the 2 pieces of fusible interfacing
lengthwise. Straight stitch them together to form 1 piece
that measures approximately 43" x 43". You may want to
cut this piece to 35" x 43" so that it is the same size as
the freezer paper. This will be $^1/_2$" larger on all sides
than the outline fabric.

3. Use your favorite method to enlarge the pattern on
page 68 by 440%. Note that this pattern is already
reversed for tracing.

4. Trace the enlarged pattern onto the dull side of the
freezer paper.

5. To temporarily adhere the freezer paper to the interfacing, lightly iron the *shiny side* of the freezer paper to
the *non-glue* side of the fusible interfacing.

6. Use a craft knife to cut through the freezer paper and
the fusible interfacing to form the lace.

7. Fuse the lace onto the wrong side of the outline fabric.

8. Remove the freezer paper.

APPLIQUÉ

*See pages 27–30 for complete instructions on how to
create the windows and appliqué.*

1. Cut out a few windows at a time leaving a $^3/_{16}$" turn-
under allowance. Make sure the windows are not next
to each other.

2. Clip as needed, turn and press the window edges to
the interfaced side.

3. Insert and glue or pin the window fabrics in place.

4. Use the monofilament thread on top and the white
thread in the bobbin. Zigzag on the right side of the
quilt top, catching both the window and outline fabrics.
Backstitch at the beginning and end to anchor the
stitches.

5. Press with an iron on a medium setting. Monofilament
thread melts at high settings.

6. Repeat, doing 3 or 4 windows at a time, until the quilt
top is complete.

Eyes

Here is an easy way to make the eyes. Feel free to design your own.

1. Iron the fusible web to the wrong side of the black and the white 4" x 4" squares.

2. Trace around the large and small black eye templates onto the black fabric. Make 3 of each. Cut out.

3. Trace around the medium white eye template onto the white fabric. Make 3. Cut out.

4. Remove the paper backing from each of the eyes.

5. Stack the eyes. The largest black eye is on the bottom, the medium white in the middle, and the smallest black on top.

Stack the eyes.

6. Place a stack on one of the locations indicated on the pattern.

7. Fuse the eyes down according to the manufacturer's instructions.

8. Repeat with the 2 remaining fish eyes.

9. You may want to stitch the eyes down for further stability.

FINISHING

See pages 35–42 for complete instructions on quilting and finishing techniques.

1. Trim, quilt, and bind the piece. Block the quilt, if desired.

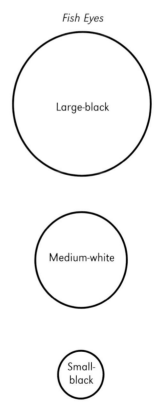

Fish Eyes

Large-black

Medium-white

Small-black

Full-size, do not enlarge.

Go Fishing

Enlarge 440%.

Pattern is already reversed for tracing.

Hovering

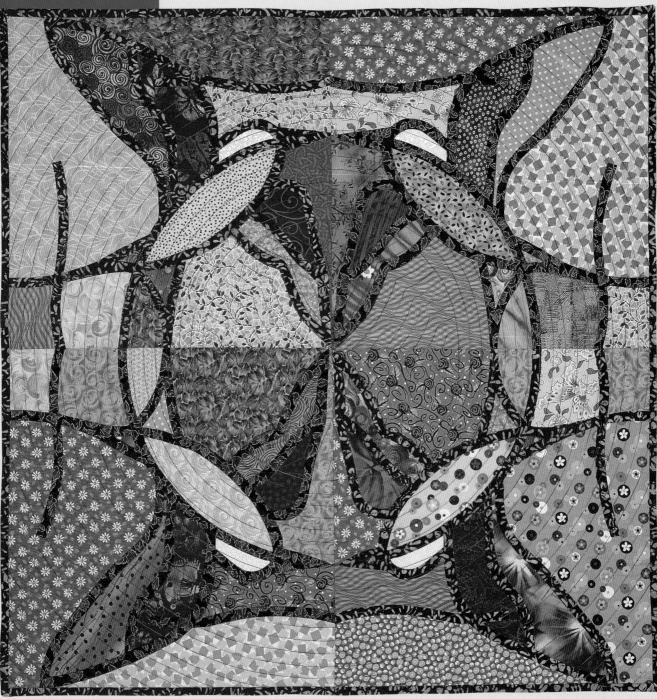

Finished quilt size: 36" x 36"

Mirror images of hummingbirds hovering in flight create a serenely balanced design. This complex-looking piece is actually a simple Four-Patch quilt. It uses only one pattern that is rotated and mirrored to form a circular flight path. The blue-patterned fabrics for the outline create a different look for this quilt. Enjoy experimenting with color choices for the outline and within each hummingbird.

MATERIALS

See page 7 for complete descriptions of tools and supplies.

Dark blue prints for outline and binding: 1½ yards

Light blue, lavender, and light green prints for background: a variety to total 1½ yards

Yellow, orange, pink, and red fabrics for birds: a variety to total ¾ yard

White fabric for bird heads: scraps

Batting: 40" x 40"

Backing: 1¼ yards

Freezer paper: 2 yards of 18"-wide

Medium-weight fusible interfacing: 2 yards of 22"-wide

Monofilament thread

Blue sewing thread for bobbin

Thread for quilting

Glue stick

Pins

Scissors for trimming fabric

Craft knife

Rotary cutter, ruler, and mat

CUTTING

Dark blue print fabric for outline: Cut 4 squares 19" x 19".

Dark blue print fabric for binding: Cut 4 strips 2¾" x width of fabric.

Freezer paper: Cut 4 squares 18" x 18".

Fusible interfacing: Cut 4 squares 18" x 18".

PREPARATION

See pages 22–26 for complete instructions on how to enlarge, trace, and create the lace.

1. Use your favorite method to enlarge the pattern on page 72 by 240%.

2. Trace the enlarged pattern, onto the dull sides of 2 pieces of freezer paper.

3. Use 1 of the traced patterns to trace the mirror image of the pattern onto the dull sides of the remaining 2 pieces of freezer paper. To trace the mirror image, flip over the previously traced pattern (shiny side up), and place against a window or on a light table. Place a blank piece of freezer paper (dull side up) on top of the traced pattern. The light from the window or light table will allow you to see the reversed image and trace it onto the dull side of the freezer paper.

Trace the pattern right side up 2 times, and the mirror image 2 times.

4. To temporarily adhere the freezer paper to the interfacing, lightly iron the *shiny side* of the freezer paper to the *non-glue* side of the fusible interfacing. Repeat for all the pieces.

5. Use a craft knife to cut through the freezer paper and the fusible interfacing to form the lace. Repeat with all the pieces.

6. Fuse the lace onto the wrong side of the outline fabric. Repeat for all the pieces.

7. Remove the freezer paper.

APPLIQUÉ

See pages 27–30 for complete instructions on how to create the windows and appliqué.

1. Cut out a few windows at a time leaving a $^3/_{16}$" turn-under allowance. Make sure the windows are not next to each other.

2. Clip as needed, turn and press the window edges to the interfaced side.

3. Insert and glue or pin a few of the window fabrics in place.

4. Use the monofilament thread on top and the blue thread in the bobbin. Zigzag on the right side of the quilt top, catching both the window and outline fabrics. Backstitch at the beginning and end to anchor the stitches.

5. Press with an iron on a medium setting. Monofilament thread melts at high settings.

6. Repeat, doing 3 or 4 windows at a time, until each section is complete.

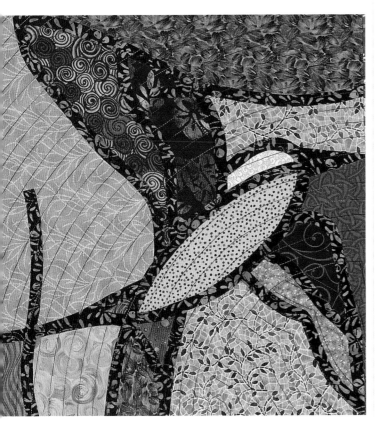

FINISHING

See pages 35–42 for complete instructions on quilting and finishing techniques.

1. Trim all the pieces to $18^1/_2$" x $18^1/_2$", centering the pattern on each piece before you trim.

2. Align the blocks using the photo on page 69 as a reference. Match the outlines and fabrics along the seams and place the right sides together. Sew using a $^1/_4$" seam allowance.

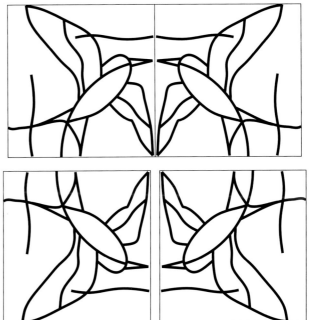

Align blocks and sew with a $^1/_4$" seam allowance.

3. Sew the blocks together in pairs. Press the seams open.

4. Sew the joined pairs together. Press the seams open.

5. Trim, quilt, and bind the piece. Block the quilt, if desired.

Hovering
Enlarge pattern 240%.

Flower Arranging

Finished quilt size: 34" x 44"

Try your hand at *Flower Arranging*. Here's a chance to make a pieced border; the graphic black and white checkerboard is the perfect frame for this bouquet of flowers. Remember to select a large variety of lavender, pink, and yellow fabrics for the petals. Each of these flowers has a number of petals, so this is the perfect place to use many different fabrics.

MATERIALS

See page 7 for complete descriptions of tools and supplies.

Black or dark colored fabric for outline, checkerboard border, and binding: 2 yards

Pink fabrics for flower and background: a variety to total $^3/_4$ yard

Light green fabrics for background: a variety to total $^3/_4$ yard

Yellow fabrics for flower: a variety to total $^1/_3$ yard

Lavender fabrics for flower: a variety to total $^1/_3$ yard

Brown fabrics for flower centers: 3 squares 10" x 10" each

Orange fabrics for vase: a variety to total $^1/_4$ yard

Black-and-white polka dot fabrics for vase: a variety to total $^1/_4$ yard

White fabric for checkerboard border: $^1/_4$ yard

Batting: 38" x 48"

Backing: 1 $^3/_8$ yards

Freezer paper: 2 $^1/_2$ yards of 18"-wide

Medium-weight fusible interfacing: 2 $^1/_2$ yards of 22"-wide

Monofilament thread

Dark sewing thread for the bobbin

Thread for quilting

Glue stick

Pins

Scissors for trimming fabric

Craft knife

Rotary cutter, ruler, and mat

CUTTING

Black or dark fabric for outline: Cut 1 rectangle 31" x 41".

Black or dark fabric for binding: Cut 5 strips 2$^3/_4$ " x width of fabric.

Black fabric for checkerboard border: Cut 6 strips 1$^1/_2$" x width of the fabric.

White fabric for checkerboard border: Cut 6 strips 1$^1/_2$" x width of the fabric.

Freezer paper: Cut 2 pieces 18" x 42".

Fusible interfacing: Cut 2 pieces 22" x 42".

PREPARATION

See pages 22–26 for complete instructions on how to enlarge, trace, and create the lace.

1. Slightly overlap the 2 pieces of freezer paper lengthwise. Secure them with transparent tape on the dull side to form 1 piece that measures approximately 35" x 42". Trim to 32" x 42".

2. Slightly overlap the 2 pieces of fusible interfacing lengthwise. Straight stitch them together to form 1 piece that measures approximately 43" x 42". You may want to cut this piece to 32" x 42" so that it is the same size as the freezer paper. This will be $^1/_2$" larger on all sides than the outline fabric.

3. Use your favorite method to enlarge the pattern on page 76 by 400%. Note that this pattern is already reversed for tracing.

4. Trace the enlarged pattern onto the dull side of the freezer paper.

5. To temporarily adhere the freezer paper to the interfacing, lightly iron the *shiny side* of the freezer paper to the *non-glue* side of the fusible interfacing.

6. Use a craft knife to cut through the freezer paper and the fusible interfacing to form the lace.

7. Fuse the lace onto the wrong side of the outline fabric.

8. Remove the freezer paper.

FLOWER CENTERS

Stitch the spiral centers of the flowers before you insert them in the window.

1. Draw the spiral pattern from the full enlargement of the pattern on page 76 onto the brown center fabrics.

2. Stabilize the wrong side of the fabric with fusible interfacing to prevent distortion.

3. Use a twin needle to slowly stitch the spiral pattern.

4. After you stitch the spiral, the fabric may be distorted. Place the fabric wrong side up and press out the distortion.

Stitch the spiral with a twin needle.

APPLIQUÉ

See pages 27–30 for complete instructions on how to create the windows and appliqué.

1. Cut out a few windows at a time leaving a $^3/_{16}$" turn-under allowance. Make sure the windows are not next to each other.

2. Turn and press the window edges to the interfaced side.

3. Insert and glue or pin the window fabrics in place.

4. Use the monofilament thread on top and the dark thread in the bobbin. Zigzag on the right side of the quilt top, catching both the window and outline fabrics. Backstitch at the beginning and end to anchor the stitches.

5. Press with an iron on a medium setting. Monofilament thread melts at high settings.

6. Repeat, doing 3 or 4 windows at a time, until the quilt top is complete.

7. Center the pattern, and trim the quilt top to measure $30^1/_2$" x $40^1/_2$".

PIECED BORDER

See pages 31–34 for complete instructions on making pieced borders.

1. Sew 1 black strip to 1 white strip together lengthwise using a $^1/_4$" seam allowance. Repeat to create a total of 6 strip sets.

2. Press all the seams toward the dark fabric.

3. Place the strip set right side up and cut into $1^1/_2$" units.

4. Sew these $1^1/_2$" units together using a $^1/_4$" seam allowance, rotating every other unit, to form a checkerboard pattern.

5. Press all the seams in one direction.

6. Make 2 checkerboard border strips that measure $40^1/_2$" for the longer sides of the quilt.

7. Make 2 checkerboard border strips that measure $34^1/_2$" for the shorter sides of the quilt.

8. Sew the longer border strips to the corresponding sides of the quilt top. Press the seams toward the borders.

9. Repeat for the shorter sides of the quilt.

FINISHING

See pages 35–42 for complete instructions on quilting and finishing techniques.

1. Trim, quilt, and bind the piece. Block the quilt, if desired.

Flower Arranging
Enlarge 400%.
Pattern is already reversed for tracing.

ABOUT THE AUTHOR

A native of New York, Julie Hirota was raised in Southern California with her younger brother and sister. She ventured up to Davis, where she attended the University of California and received dual bachelor degrees in Mechanical Engineering and Material Science Engineering. It was her experiences with clay, glass, fiber, jewelry casting, and print making at the campus craft center that led Julie to a love of art and fine craft.

Julie permanently relocated to the basin of the Sierra Foothills in 1993 for her first professional career assignment in Mechanical Engineering. At the same time, she met and married her husband, Aaron, also a Davis graduate in Mechanical Engineering. Today, the two enjoy gardening, hiking, and spending time with their daughter and their pets, 3 cats and a dog.

During her engineering career, Julie's fiber art was supposedly a part-time passion but she spent many sleepless nights creating. After leaving the high-tech industry, Julie discovered the lifestyle fulfillment of artistic expression and decided to pursue art as a full-time career.

Julie exhibits primarily at fine art shows and festivals throughout California. Between shows she lectures, teaches, and creates commissions for residential and corporate clients. Her work can also be found in national exhibits and publications. Visit her website at www.jhiro.com for her complete exhibition and travel schedule.

INDEX

RESOURCES

Supplies

Quilting Supplies:

Cotton Patch Mail Order,
3404 Hall Lane, Dept. CTB,
Lafayette, CA 94549
800-835-4418, 925-283-7883
email: quiltusa@yahoo.com
website: www.quiltusa.com

Shirt Tailor, Pellon Interfacing:

Available at Jo-Ann's, Hancock
Fabrics, and other fabric stores

Pattern Drafting Paper:

Apparel City Sewing Machine,
1330 Howard St.
San Francisco, CA
415-621-6660, 800-613-6660

Note: Fabrics used in the quilts shown may not be currently available because fabric manufacturers keep most fabrics in print for only a short time.

Color and Design Books

Color: The Quilter's Guide by Christine Barnes

Complex Cloth by Jane Dunnewold

The Quilters Book of Design, Color by Accident, and *Color by Design* by Anne Johnston

Skydyes by Micky Lawler

Dyeing to Quilt by Joyce Mori and Cynthia Myerberg

Fabric Stamping Handbook by Jean Ray Laury

Other Fine Books from C&T Publishing

15 Two-Block Quilts: Unlock the Secrets of Secondary Patterns, Claudia Olson

24 Quilted Gems: Sparkling Traditional & Original Projects, Gai Perry

250 Continuous-Line Quilting Designs for Hand, Machine & Long-Arm Quilters, Laura Lee Fritz

250 More Continuous-Line Quilting Designs for Hand, Machine & Long-Arm Quilters, Laura Lee Fritz

All About Machine Arts—Decorative Techniques from A to Z, From Sew News Creative Machine Embroidery & C&T Publishing

All About Quilting from A to Z, From the Editors and Contributors of *Quilter's Newsletter Magazine* and *Quiltmaker* Magazine

America's Printed Fabrics 1770–1890: 8 Reproduction Quilt Projects ·Hitoric Notes & Photographs · Dating Your Quilts, Barbara Brackman

An Amish Adventure, 2nd Edition: A Workbook for Color in Quilts, Roberta Horton

Anatomy of a Doll: The Fabric Sculptor's Handbook, Susanna Oroyan

Appliqué 12 Easy Ways!: Charming Quilts, Giftable Projects & Timeless Techniques, Elly Sienkiewicz

Appliqué Delights: 100 Irresistible Blocks from Piece O' Cake Designs, Becky Goldsmith & Linda Jenkins

Appliqué Inside the Lines: 12 Quilt Projects to Embroider & Appliqué, Carol Armstrong

Art Glass Quilts: New Subtractive Appliqué Technique, Julie Hirotas

Art of Classic Quiltmaking, The, Harriet Hargrave & Sharyn Craig

Art of Machine Piecing, The: How to Achieve Quality Workmanship Through a Colorful Journey,
Sally Collins

Artful Ribbon, The: Beauties in Bloom, Candace Kling

At Piece With Time: A Woman's Journey Stitched in Cloth, Kristin Steiner & Diane Frankenberger

Beading Basics: 30 Embellishing Techniques for Quilters, Mary Stori

Beautifully Quilted with Alex Anderson: · How to Choose or Create the Best Designs for Your Quilt · 5 Timeless Projects · Full-size Patterns, Ready to Use, Alex Anderson

Benni Harper's Quilt Album: A Scrapbook of Quilt Projects, Photos & Never-Before-Told Stories, Earlene Fowler & Margrit Hall

Best of Baltimore Beauties, The: 95 Patterns for Album Blocks and Borders, Elly Sienkiewicz

Best of Baltimore Beauties Part II, The: More Patterns for Album Blocks, Elly Sienkiewicz

Block Magic: Over 50 Fun & Easy Blocks from Squares and Rectangles, Nancy Johnson-Srebro

Block Magic, Too!: Over 50 NEW Blocks from Squares and Rectangles, Nancy Johnson-Srebro

Borders, Bindings & Edges: The Art of Finishing Your Quilt, Sally Collins

Butterflies & Blooms: Designs for Appliqué & Quilting, Carol Armstrong

Cats in Quilts: 14 Purrfect Projects, Carol Armstrong

Celebrate Great Quilts! circa 1820–1940: The International Quilt Festival Collection, Karey Patterson Bresenhan & Nancy O'Bryant

Celebrate the Tradition with C&T Publishing: Over 70 Fabulous New Blocks, Tips & Stories from Quilting's Best, C&T Staff

Circle Play: Simple Designs for Fabulous Fabrics, Reynola Pakusich

Color Play: Easy Steps to Imaginative Color in Quilts, Joen Wolfrom

Contemporary Classics in Plaids & Stripes: 9 Projects from Piece 'O Cake Designs, Linda Jenkins & Becky Goldsmith

Country Quilts for Friends: 18 Charming Projects for All Seasons, Margaret Peters & Anne Sutton

Crazy Quilt Handbook, The: Revised, 2nd Edition, Judith Baker Montano

Curl-Up Quilts: Flannel Appliqué & More from Piece O' Cake Designs, Becky Goldsmith & Linda Jenkins

Cut-Loose Quilts: Stack, Slice, Switch, and Sew, Jan Mullen

Dolls of the Art Deco Era 1910–1940: Collect, Restore, Create & Play, Susanna Oroyan

Elegant Stitches: An Illustrated Stitch Guide & Source Book of Inspiration, Judith Baker Montano

Elm Creek Quilts: Quilt Projects Inspired by the Elm Creek Quilts Novels, Jennifer Chiaverini & Nancy Odom

Enchanted Views: Quilts Inspired by Wrought-Iron Designs, Dilys Fronks

Endless Possibilities: Using No-Fail Methods, Nancy Johnson-Srebro

Fantastic Fabric Folding: Innovative Quilting Projects, Rebecca Wat

Fantastic Fans: Exquisite Quilts & Other Projects, Alice Dunsdon

Fast, Fun & Easy Fabric Bowls: 5 Reversible Shapes to Use & Display, Linda Johansen

For more information, ask for a free catalog:

C&T Publishing, Inc.

P.O. Box 1456

Lafayette, CA 94549

(800) 284-1114

Email: ctinfo@ctpub.com

Website: www.ctpub.com